Lottie TOMLINSON

LUCKY GIRL

Lottie
TOMLINSON

LUCKY GIRL
Family, Falling and Finding my Way

BLINK
bringing you closer

Lottie Tomlinson is one of the UK's most in demand influencers with a following of 4.9 million and a market leading tanning brand (Tanologist) that she launched at just 19. She has pioneered beauty trends and worked with everyone from Dior Beauty and Givenchy to ASOS and Boux Avenue.

After losing her mother and sister and experiencing first-hand the impact of grief and the lack of support available to young people, Lottie became a passionate supporter of causes relating to mental health. Lottie is a patron of bereavement charity Sue Ryder and has spoken in parliament alongside Dr Rosena Allin-Khan MP about shaping policies to provide more access to grief counselling.

In 2022 Lottie became a mother to her son, Lucky Burton.

First published in the UK by Blink Publishing
An imprint of The Zaffre Publishing Group
A Bonnier Books UK company
4th Floor, Victoria House
Bloomsbury Square,
London, WC1B 4DA
England

Owned by Bonnier Books
Sveavägen 56, Stockholm, Sweden

Instagram: @blinkpublishing
X: @blinkpublishing

First published in 2024

Hardback – 9781785121128
Trade Paperback – 9781785121166
eBook – 9781785121142
Audio Digital Download – 9781785121159

British Library Cataloguing-in-Publication Data:

A catalogue record for this book is available from the British Library.

Designed by Envy Design Ltd
Printed and bound in Great Britain by Clays Ltd, Elcograf S.p.A.

1 3 5 7 9 10 8 6 4 2

Blink Publishing is an imprint of Bonnier Books UK
www.bonnierbooks.co.uk

To my mum & Fizz for inspiring me every day,
I love you both forever.

To my beautiful boys, you make me
feel lucky every day.

CONTENTS

FOREWORD

I first thought about Lottie doing influencer work for my agency, The Book, while I was sitting on the set of a One Direction music video, discussing Lottie with one of Louis' managers. I told her Lottie had real potential, that I could see her doing well. I told her about Lottie's huge Instagram following, how cute and commercial she was, how we'd landed her first gig, how we planned to work with other brands and launch new projects.

Some time after that conversation, Lottie told me that her brother's management had offered her representation, and I just said, 'Look, this is business. It's not personal, so you do what's right for you.' I knew Louis had the biggest managers ever, and that they were very good, but Lottie just said, 'I think you see it in me, and I want to do it with you.'

Right from the beginning, she'd given me that bit of loyalty, and it made me want to back her through everything. We'd always been a team, since touring together with One Direction (Lottie was my hair and makeup assistant). When Lottie cares about someone, she wants to do right by them, and on tour she was my emotional support and my best friend. But her decision to stick with my agency cemented our relationship and said so much about who she was by the age of 18. She wanted to be comfortable and she could see that the two of us would be long-term.

While Lottie was like a little sister to me on tour, I was sometimes like a mother to her. But that's not something she needs from me now. She has a sharp business mind and works hard, so that others take her seriously. But she combines that professionalism with a very caring and soft side.

There's no ego with Lottie. We've been on influencer trips together where girls from reality TV shows are swanning down for an early meet half an hour late, but Lottie's always punctual and would never behave like that. Sometimes she'll say things and I'll remember how old she is, but because of her family background, and now her business responsibilities, she's used to looking after people and is very mature for her years. Lottie's never thinking about herself or trying to take ownership of what's hers. She's always about everybody else.

As a hair and makeup artist, I've worked with a lot of celebrities and most of them are so guarded, but that's not Lottie. She used to be so embarrassed having her pictures taken, but now we'll be in Ibiza and she'll be getting the shot and not caring. She's confident now, because she's comfortable with who she is.

Sometimes at promo gigs, the press will want to talk about Louis or Lewis instead of what she's there to promote – Tanologist or her work with the charity Sue Ryder, projects she's proud of. But those questions don't make her uncomfortable or stress her out, instead she just deals with them and moves on. Lottie's got a very thick skin, so it would be quite difficult to upset her now.

The Tomlinson kids succeed in anything they put their minds to, and it's amazing to see Lottie and her sister Phoebe with their little babies. At such a young age, the girls are taking it all in their stride and are the cutest little mums. If the kids are going crazy, they don't flinch. Instead, they're nurturing and calm. And you can tell they're loving it because they're always so gushing about motherhood, always laughing and never complaining.

When Louis came to Lucky's first birthday party, which was a house full of kids, he said, 'This is what our first house was like, and Lottie's recreated it.' After everything that's happened with them, their worlds are not dark at all. And it's clear that they appreciate everything.

Their mum Jay was soft and kind but also took no shit. I could see those traits in Louis when I first started working for him and now I can see them in Lottie. Everything they do is about family and they're incredibly generous in how they treat people whether it's a night out or a holiday. That's a big part of why Lottie and Louis work so hard, so that they can share the enjoyment. It's a beautiful thing to watch.

Lottie and I are very funny with each other these days. We'll send each other gushy texts every now and again, even though we're actually quite British and won't usually say how we feel. But even without those gushy texts, she knows how I feel about her and that I'll always be here for her, just like she's always there for other people in her life.

Love,
Lou Teasdale

PROLOGUE

I'm enjoying a more stripped-back life now-adays. It's a more stripped-back me as well. My confidence has grown these last few years and now I understand what it means to live a more balanced life.

It's the simple things that make me happiest, like being with my partner, Lewis, and my little boy, Lucky. I love waking up in our new home and doing the everyday, like making Lucky breakfast and watching him enjoy it. I love it when the three of us wake up with bedhead, before moving to the sofa and sitting there looking all cute and scruffy. Those moments might not seem like much but they're just for us.

After all I've been through these past seven years, I sometimes can't believe that this is my life. When I lost my mum and sister, I thought I'd never live a happy life again. I genuinely thought it was over, that it would be filled with nothing but sadness, but as the years went by, I started to understand that grief doesn't have to ruin your life. It will never be the same after the grief I've experienced, but it's more beautiful than I ever thought possible. It's shocking to think about how quickly things can change from one moment to the next, but every day I count my blessings because I know what it feels like to lose the people I love the most and have my world crumble. To have created a family and home of my own gives me so much joy and so much hope. It's not something I take lightly.

When I was 15 years old, all I ever did was moan about being *so exhausted*. Now I want to say to that version of myself, 'You don't know what tired means!' But I love the work I've created, and the way I spend my days. My influencing work has given me a lot of freedom, allowing me to pick and choose what I want to do, which fits in perfectly with Lucky. I'm also building up my wellness venture, Verdure, creating content, attending photoshoots and meetings, as well as working out, which is great for both my body and my mental health. Over the years, I've realised how important it is to make that time and space for this in my life. Staying active and having a routine has helped me get through the hardest moments of my life, although these days it's simply a part of what I do to feel strong – physically and emotionally.

Even though I'm focusing more on fashion and fitness now, makeup is still my core passion and my favourite thing to work on. From that first moment I watched Mum apply her products, I became obsessed with makeup. And I've never stopped loving how I express myself through makeup and watching that transformation process. I learned the trade through YouTube, found the courage to film my own videos, and was soon putting makeup on models during London Fashion Week. It's fair to say my fascination with beauty has been its own separate journey, one that's taken me to crazy and unexpected places. Even now when I get ready for a night out and do a full glam makeup look, I love it. It's my favourite part of getting ready. I also love filming and sharing my videos on TikTok and Instagram. Some of you will have seen my videos – I love filming them and sharing a bit of my life, connecting with you all and teaching what I know in the process.

It's only really in the last few years that I've settled into myself and who I am. I can enjoy the natural and the everyday, yet still embrace those other parts of me you see on social media, like those glammed-up photos, nice trips and evenings out.

It's all a bit of fun, but I know it's not what happiness is all about. I've always enjoyed creating and posting content, it's something I've done for a long time way before Instagram took off. But I've come a long way from the 16-year-old who struggled a bit with her weight. I was young and insecure back then, and starting up on social media got me playing games of comparison with the girls I saw online. I'll always be grateful for social media though – it's given me this amazing career, enabling me to earn money I never thought I'd earn as someone who grew up with not too much, so I don't like talking too negatively about it – but the truth is I'd see these girls and think, *I don't have a waist like that … I don't have skin like that … I don't have this or that … By* the time filler culture came in, I thought, *Right, I'm gonna do these fillers and I'm gonna feel confident like these other girls.* But soon I discovered it didn't give me the confidence I was looking for.

Like so many, I chased a dream, convincing myself I needed just a bit more to achieve the results that I wanted. When that didn't work, I thought what I needed to do was eat less and train more, but I was never good enough. That's partly a natural part of being a teenage girl and growing up, but a lot of it was heightened due to my work online.

After the journey I've been on, I can see now that happiness is not all about material things, like going to the best events, wearing the best clothes, or looking perfect. Don't get me wrong, I love all those things, but I went through stages of needing every beauty treatment, of needing to be as skinny as possible, of needing the big lips, the big lashes and all the makeup, and that's a lot to keep up with. These days, it's a relief not trying to be perfect all the time, and I can see the beauty in the imperfections too. But these are lessons I've had to learn the hard way.

I've gone through a lot in only a few years. My mum Johannah died when I was 18 years old, and that had a huge impact on my confidence. I lost the one person who loved me unconditionally and who had always been around to give me reassurance and support. I remember Mum telling me I didn't need the treatments – not in a forceful way, Mum was always soft and gentle – and encouraging me not to do too much because she thought I was beautiful the way I was. She was special like that, the best kind of mum, and I miss her and her warmth so much. And I never forgot her advice, even when I found it difficult to follow it.

When I became pregnant with Lucky in 2021, I knew I wouldn't be able to have any treatments. At first, I was a little worried because I'd relied on them so much, but it turned out to be the best thing for me – in so many ways. After I gave birth, I decided it was time to dissolve the fillers. My lips were black from the bruising – quite honestly, the whole process is pain, whether you're putting the fillers in or taking them away –

but the strange thing was that removing the fillers helped me accept who I am and how I look, and I instantly felt better about myself. It makes me sad when I look at pictures of me with all that stuff in my face. And while I spent a lot of money and went through a lot of pain to get rid of those fillers, I feel so much better for doing so.

In a way, it's a shame. But in another way, it's also part of my journey, so I don't want to judge myself harshly. I needed to go through the experience to better understand myself. I still love getting dressed up, doing my makeup and having my hair extensions done, but I have a much healthier relationship with how I look now. I'm happy to wake up and have a day with no makeup and wearing my scruffs, and I couldn't have said that even just a few years ago.

Trying to be comfortable in your skin is easier said than done; it's a long process, and an up and down journey. I'm now in a place where I feel truly happy, but it's taken me a while to get here. When loss and grief hit you it can change your life forever, but I've learned how to navigate those hard times. So if any of you reading this are going through hard times, I really hope this book helps. Please believe me when I say the hard times will diminish over time.

It might sound odd to say it, but I consider myself lucky, just as my mum did before she passed away. It was Mum who encouraged me to go after my dreams even when I didn't know exactly what those were. I've been putting my life out to the public since I was so young, but I don't feel like I've ever given people a proper insight into my story. Now that I'm more at ease, especially after the love that's come into my life since having Lucky, I'm ready to take you on that journey with me. I can't promise that I'll provide you with all the answers, because sadly that's not how life works, and I can't provide you with magic tools to make it all better; but I can show you that it's possible to do more than just survive, and that there's help along the way.

Behind all the pain I've experienced there's been a lot of hope and a lot of light. And one thing I've come to realise is that everything revolves around love – whether you're in love, whether you're going through heartbreak, whether you're trying to find love, everyone has some association with it. Love honestly makes the world go round. I've been through all of those stages. I've been in love. I'm in love now, with both my partner and my little boy, which is just an amazing feeling. I've also had my heart broken by the loss of my mum and my litter sister Fizz. And even when I've dealt with heartbreak, I've always had the love of my amazing family – my mum and dad, my nan and granddad, my sisters Fizz, Phoebe, Daisy and Doris, and my brothers Louis and Ernie. Because of that love, I've learned that you can come through the darkest times of your life even when you don't think you can. I've used those painful moments as fuel to create something I'm proud and happy of. It's not been easy to revisit the pain of the last few years, but I know it's important for me to do so, as a celebration of how far I've truly come.

CHAPTER ONE

It's hardly surprising that I grew up baby mad, because I was surrounded by them from a young age. First Mum brought home my sister Félicité (Fizz), then Phoebe and Daisy (the big twins), and later Doris and Ernie (the little twins).

From what Nan has told me, Mum was quite a mischievous kid who ran rings round her and Granddad. She then fell pregnant with Louis at the age of 18 – about the same age Phoebe was when she had her little girl Olive, who we've just welcomed into our family.

It's possible that Mum was such a handful as a child because of the tragic death of her older brother Jonathan, who was killed in an accident when he was just three years old. Mum was only 15 months at the time, but it must've had a traumatic effect on her.

Over time, Mum would become easier to manage, and Nan would go on to have another child, my aunty Rachael, but such a sad situation would've no doubt affected them all. I sometimes wonder if Mum's passion for children had anything to do with her brother's passing, especially from what Nan tells me about her. Whenever they went away on holiday and Mum disappeared, they'd find the nearest family with children and that's where Mum would be. Mum needed children around her all the time, which is probably why she went on to have the seven of us.

Even though Mum fell pregnant young – which was obviously hard for my Nan and Granddad, who were quite traditional and wanted their daughter to finish schooling – she went on to train as a midwife and have a successful career. Mum always knew what she wanted, which was to help bring life into this world, and she wasn't going to stop until she got there.

Although she was very determined, Nan says that Mum tended to do everything a different way round to most people, such as doing her four-year midwifery degree while trying to look after three children. Nan and Granddad were always around to help, but there were so many times when Mum would be up all night studying. I honestly don't know how she did it, she was incredible.

Nan and Grandad's house had a study covered in

textbooks and with Post-it notes all over the walls. And things got so tough towards the end of her degree that she told Nan and Grandad that she didn't think she could carry on. Apparently, Granddad told her, 'Jay [her name was Johannah but that's what her parents called her], you're nearly there, keep going, keep going.' They were in awe of her, doing all that studying while looking after three kids, and Nan says that's where we get our determination from. Whenever any of us kids wants to do something, we go ahead and do it to the best of our ability.

Before I had dreams of pursuing makeup, I wanted to be a midwife purely because Mum did it. She used to let us come into the maternity ward with her so we could have a look at the babies and hold them. Afterwards, we'd follow her to the back room where they kept the baby bottles that they gave new mums, and she'd even let us take a few home for our dolls. I was so young, so I never thought about having to go through medical training or even having to deliver the babies. For me, it was just getting to see babies every day that made me happy.

We grew up in Doncaster, in a little village called Bessacarr. Home was a three-bedroom house that would soon be far too small for the size of our family. Mum moved there with my brother Louis in 1998 as a single mum, before I was born, and my soon-to-be dad lived right next door. As Dad tells the story, their eyes met as Mum was moving all her gear in and it was love at first sight. Less than eight months later, Dad moved in with her and Louis and not long after that they were married.

Mum and Dad married young, and their wedding photos are so precious. In one photo, they're looking into each other's eyes as they cut the cake. Dad has dark, shoulder-length hair; he's wearing round spectacles and a dark suit with a big burgundy tie tucked into the front. As for Mum, she's got a big smile on her face and looks so sweet and radiant. In another photo, she's posing with a bouquet of red and white roses inside the church. She's also wearing a crown of red and white roses on her head, plus pearls paired with a beautiful white off the shoulder dress, with cute bowties on the sleeves. Absolutely stunning. When I look at those photos it reminds me of happy times with her, even though I'm not in them. It's a bitter-sweet feeling but I'll cherish those photos forever.

Nan says that when I was born, Louis cried when he held me for the first time (to be fair, he had waited seven and a half years for another sibling to come along!). Because of the age difference, Louis had his own room in the Bessacarr house, while I shared a room with Fizz, who came along two years after me, and eventually the big twins Phoebe and Daisy. I was six when they were born in 2004, and obviously Fizz and I were so excited. And because there were two new babies, we didn't have to fight over them (the big twins felt the same way when Doris and Ernie were born in 2014).

Having a big family comes with a lot of noise, so I had to be quite determined if I wanted to be heard. But Nan says I was very helpful, and she remembers me at the age of six casually walking around with a baby on my hip. I have lovely memories of my childhood at this time. We all went to a nice school around the corner from the house, and on our way home we'd go to the local village shop to buy a 20p worth of 'pick and mix' sweets. That was such a highlight of our day.

For the summer holidays we'd all jump into our seven-seater car and drive to one of those Keycamp caravan resorts in the south of France. We wouldn't sleep the night before because of how excited we were – we looked forward to those holidays so much. Dad would spend most of his time in the pool and Fizz would be at the kids' club or meeting a new family – you wouldn't see her for the whole holiday. Every summer Mum tried to put me in the kids' club to socialise, but I'd never want to go. I'd spend all my time crying because all I wanted was to stay with my family. Being close to my mum and having all my siblings around me was everything I needed. Why would I want to make new friends?

It's funny to think back to those times because I'm

definitely more sociable now. I've found my confidence and am less nervous and reserved in social situations. Even so, I'm not really one to bring just anyone into my life, and my inner circle of friends is quite small.

Eventually, the four of us girls shared a room, all of us sleeping in two separate bunk beds. Our life was fun and chaotic back then, but I loved it. We had a few dogs too, who added to the craziness. As everyone always says, Mum was very soft, so when we begged her for dogs, she eventually gave in, even though none of us had time to train them. We had to re-home a couple of them because it was just too much for us to handle.

Even though Mum had loads of responsibilities to juggle in those days, nothing was ever too much for her. She really was the centre of our world. Mum seemed to be able to do it all, from midwifery to parenting, and she dedicated everything to us, which is something I'm so lucky to have experienced. Every time we'd go to her with a problem, she'd be there for us. And she had us in every club because she wanted us to figure out what we enjoyed. We used to dance, play football, go to gymnastics. Whatever it was, she encouraged us to be ambitious and to follow our passions, just like she did.

We didn't have a lot of money back then, which meant Mum having to rotate the same few outfits while she constantly bought us new things. Don't get me wrong, we never went without, but there were so many of us and not enough money to go around. Sometimes money was so tight we couldn't afford to top up the meter key for electricity, so we all lit candles and played games. We didn't really need the telly because we had each other. Those times seem so far away, but they're still some of my favourite memories. It was all of us sticking together and mucking in.

It's mind-blowing to think about how many of us there were. Louis was your typical older brother, a bit of a wind-up merchant but very loving and protective. He had sister after sister come in and that's hard for any big brother, but he was always brilliant with us.

For as long as I can remember, Louis spent his time singing a lot and being musical. Most of the time, he'd be out with friends or playing in his band. Fizz, on the other hand, was different to the rest of us. She was *really* smart, unique, outspoken and opinionated – in fact, she was almost too intelligent for her own good.

Fizz never had to try and get As, whereas I struggled academically. She also had the biggest heart, the kindest soul, and would do anything for us. Even though we were only two years apart, Fizz looked up to me as her big sister. But we also had a bit of sisterly rivalry going on. As a child, I felt like Fizz was trying to steal my light all the time, always wanting to do the same activities as me and constantly stealing my clothes and toys. At the time, I couldn't see it all for what it was, so we'd end up fighting about something silly like her trying to play with me when I didn't want my little sister involved. But as soon as we got put in separate rooms, we'd talk through the vents in the floor (Mum didn't realise that we could see each other through them). And as we grew older, we became best friends. Meanwhile, the big twins, Phoebe and Daisy, had each other. They were just naughty, even as babies. I remember hearing about how they used to switch their name tags at nursery, and no one being able to tell them apart because they were so identical.

As a toddler, I had a fringe, cut straight across my forehead, and a little blonde bob that accentuated my big blue eyes which probably took up most of my face for a while. It's so funny when I look back at photos of us all. It brings so many memories flooding back. As a kid growing up, I was determined at home, but never fit in with others at school and found it hard to make friends. Believe it or not, I was quite shy and struggled with my confidence, and when I started Year 7, I had a bit of what you'd probably call 'puppy fat'. I certainly wasn't happy with how I looked.

I've always found it hard letting people in, mostly because I'm quite guarded. It's even true for my life now – there are a lot of acquaintances, and I generally get on with people, but I only have a handful of true friends and will only pursue relationships if they feel right.

On a deeper level, most won't get my full energy unless I really feel a connection, and I struggle to relate to most people. Sometimes, I wish I could be more forthcoming, the way my partner Lewis is. He has a big group of people around him and can make friends with anyone. I love that about him, but I can meet someone and know straightaway that we'll never develop a deep friendship. Lewis tells me not to be so quick to judge, but for me it's an instinct, something I had to learn after Louis found fame. When your schoolmates all of a sudden see you in a different light, and people start wanting to be your friend, you learn to be a bit more cautious about who you let in. It takes me a while to build that trust with people. They really have to earn it.

For a while, I had a small group of friends that I kind of just fell into, and because I was quiet, no one else noticed me. The other kids around me, many of them way more outgoing, quite easily got stuck in with a group. The girls who were considered more popular were confident. They looked good and were into their sports and lessons, whereas I was still finding my way. Around Year 8, when I was about 12 years old and Louis went onto *The X Factor* and became famous, those same girls suddenly wanted to know me. I remember the change feeling abrupt and weird but not something that bothered me too much. I know it's fickle, really, but if anything, I probably just enjoyed being more respected by people at school, even if I had to answer all these annoying questions about my brother from kids I'd never even spoken to before.

I had no idea just how much our lives were going to change. I used to take a coach to school because the drive was quite far, and as soon as I'd get on, everyone would be asking me about Louis. I even remember a few of the lads at school shouting stuff at me in the corridor, like, 'Let's roll out the red carpet!' which I just found embarrassing. When I started rolling with the 'cool' crew, I did wonder if they liked me for me. I'm quite a good judge of character these days, so I can quickly tell if someone's interested in me because my brother's famous or because I have a lot of followers on Instagram, or if it's because they genuinely want to be friends and get to know me. But back then I was young and looked up to these kids, so I didn't think about it too much.

Over time, I started to recognise who was real and who was fake. In fact, I'm still friends with a few of those girls today, including my best friend Brits, who I've known since secondary school. From the moment Brits and I met, it was like we were always meant to be friends. We just had an instant connection, and I've never met anyone else since that I've felt that with.

Before we formed our friendship, she thought of me as someone who was dead quiet, but we got close on a school ski trip to Italy when we were 13. Brits and I were put in the same room with a friend of hers and a friend of mine. I still have this vivid memory of Brits having this bag of makeup and putting on foundation in the bathroom. I just thought she was so cool. It feels weird to say that now because I've been teaching her how to put makeup on for years, but back then she was just so funny, confident and outgoing, the type of girl who loved chatting to all the boys. It was almost like she was already a proper teenager whereas I was still a little girl.

It shouldn't really have worked but Brits and I have been inseparable since school and never once fallen out. She's still the life and soul of the party, the most crazy, wild person, and someone who has been a constant throughout all the ups and downs of my life. And now we're both experiencing motherhood together, which has been so special.

*

While Mum was on night shifts, I'd hold the fort at home with Dad, who worked an office job during the day. I'd cook a bit of food for Fizz, Phoebe and Daisy and keep them entertained with games. If Mum was on a day shift, and Dad was at work, my great nanny on my granddad's side would look after us, as she and Great Granddad lived within walking distance.

My great nanny was a big part of our family and was able to help cook and feed us because she was retired by then. But I liked helping out, and it came quite naturally. When it came time to focus on my studies, however, I struggled. Mum wanted to get me into a grammar school, and to help me do that, she rented a property in the catchment area even though she didn't have a lot of money. It probably sounds a bit dodgy, but I've heard from other people that their parents were doing the same. Inspectors carried out random checks on the property, so we all used to spend weekends there, and for us kids the change of scene was quite exciting.

Mum just wanted to make sure I had the best education, but I'd never been very academic. Honestly, being in school made me feel thick. Subjects like maths used to jumble in my head and I struggled to get stuff to stick. I never had a problem getting good grades in art though, and the validation I used to receive made me feel like I was at least good at something. I'm not saying I was Picasso by any means, but I had some talent at least. Nan also used to praise my work, which was a lot coming from her because she's an amazing artist.

Nothing I was learning in school compared to how I felt about makeup. I noticed myself becoming more and more obsessed with it, while at the same time becoming less and less interested in school, wondering what studying algebra was going to do for me. I'd watch

YouTube videos and practise on my sisters in my free time. However, it never occurred to me that I could turn that into a serious career, so in the meantime I struggled with school, thinking that was my only avenue towards making something of myself. And it took me a while to realise that there are different kinds of brains: some absorb information well, and some don't, and that's okay; some brains are more suited to maths and science, while others are more suited to the arts. But when I was at school, I felt like something was wrong with me because I wasn't excelling in all of it, whereas I should have been allowed to focus on my natural gifts and interests. It's sad how one way of learning can put a lot of kids on the wrong foot, creating lots of self-doubt like it did for me.

Come exam time, I'd go in feeling quite confident sometimes, but then my mind would go blank. It seemed unfair that I was being judged on that one exam and I'd crumble under the pressure, so I didn't get the best grades. I remember my teachers recognising that I wasn't doing very well in subjects like maths, so I used to get offered extra support, like classes on the side. But even when I was taking foundation maths, for example, I still couldn't achieve a passing grade, which made me feel worse about myself.

It was tough at the time, but I can see it in a different light now. I might not have been able to sit down and do algebra but look what I've achieved. I must have some kind of intelligence? Luckily, I had my mum around to show me that just because I wasn't succeeding at school didn't mean I wouldn't succeed at all, but I imagine a lot of kids don't have that kind of support, someone telling them that it's all about finding the path that's right for you; that it's about paying attention to your passions and obsessions. Do that, and maybe you can turn what you love into a profession or a trade.

Even though I was shy, I was quite the girly girl. I loved wearing crop tops that were too small for me, and instantly became fascinated by makeup. Watching Mum put her products on, I'd want to know what each individual item did. Even though my memory has suffered from the grief and so many memories from my childhood are blurred, I have this really vivid image of looking at a liquid highlighter, putting it on my hand and asking Mum, 'What's this for?', and her explaining how she used it to raise up or accentuate certain areas of her face. *Wow, that's amazing*, I thought. Then I'd pick up a bronzer and ask, 'What does this do?', and she'd reply, 'This is gonna make you look more tanned.' I was fascinated by how makeup could transform you, how it could change your whole mood and improve your confidence. I'd spend hours on the family computer, researching makeup brands' websites. I knew all the different shades –

someone could show me a Mac lipstick and I'd know what it was called.

Benefit was a brand I was interested in at the time, and I must've been twelve when Mum said I could buy one item from them. I couldn't believe it, I thought I was the luckiest girl in the world. Mum usually let us experiment with a little lip gloss or a little bit of mascara, so I chose a concealer the brand used to do called Erase Paste, which came in a little purple pot. Mum didn't really have the money to buy something like that, but she could clearly see how interested I was in makeup. And I can still see myself scraping that concealer down right into the corners, literally getting every last bit.

I'd been able to have my makeup done during dance shows, but there was something different about having my own little product. On nights when I couldn't get to sleep, I used to think, *Right, just close your eyes and imagine that you're going into the makeup store. You can pick anything you want...* Then I'd imagine picking out all the stuff I wanted, before finally falling asleep. Maybe it sounds silly, but it was such a support for me.

Once I found that love for makeup at around 12 years old, all I wanted to do with my free time over the next several years was watch YouTube tutorials and practise on my sisters, who sometimes were like, 'Oh my god, again?' I used to beg them to let me do their makeup after school, and that's how I taught myself everything

I know. Fast-forward a few years, to right before I started touring, and I'd managed to build a little makeup collection of my own. I'd also joined Instagram for fun and was posting the occasional outfit picture when a brand called Love Co must've seen my posts about their products and paid me to post more. It wouldn't have been much, but I loved the responsibility, and it was nice to be paid.

I'd go in the garden and shoot pictures for the brand, and because this was way before I was ever managed by anyone, I must've come up with the deal myself. I then used the money they paid me to buy all these different palettes, so I could have all the colours in one place. From practising, I discovered I had a natural flare for it, which made sense as I'd always been arty. It felt like a nice way to build on my creativity in a way that I absolutely loved. My confidence soared when I was doing makeup. It excited me and made me feel good about myself, and I loved how quickly I could pick up the techniques I learned. Whereas school often upset me, and made me feel less than, makeup gave me a sense of purpose and a passion.

I never did a professional course or anything like that, I just picked up tips from the YouTube channels of makeup artists. At the time there were Samantha and Nicola Chapman, sisters who had a popular channel called 'Pixiwoo' and who went on to promote and develop a successful brushes and makeup tools brand called Real Techniques. The Chapman sisters were really good at breaking down techniques and making it all seem so simple, and off the back of 'Pixiwoo' I found the influencer Tanya Burr. I'd be buzzing some years later when Tanya invited me to make a video with her!

Through these women, I learned a lot of basic skills, not only stuff like where exactly to put concealer, but also how to do tutorials properly. Anyone can get in front of a camera and apply a lipstick, with the assumption that viewers know how to do that just by watching you, but the Chapman sisters and Tanya Burr showed me the importance of breaking down each and every step. I began to understand that the people watching the videos might not know *anything* about makeup, so an artist had to explain that with foundation, for example, using a brush gets you the most flawless finish, and blending it over and over again works it into the skin, giving you a very natural look. For the viewer to understand and achieve that professional look, an artist had to go into fine detail with each step, and that's something I'd have to eventually learn if I was going to start doing videos.

These were exciting times, and as I said earlier, it's one of the reasons why I don't knock social media, because you can learn quite a lot online. Of course social media has its negatives, but there are also lots of positives, such as all the knowledge you can find. Just by watching

YouTube videos, I became a self-taught makeup artist, although I also needed the belief and support of other people along the way.

For the most part, life was simple in those days, but like any family, things weren't always so perfect. Growing up, Dad had a drinking problem, although I think it's more accurate to say that he was struggling with an addiction or a disease, something none of us could understand at the time, not even himself.

There were times when dad was very hands-on, times when he played with us, but there were also times when he'd be drunk and argue with Mum. It was only a matter of time before things spiralled out of control and my parents divorced when I was 13.

Louis and I, being the two eldest, were probably the most aware of what was happening between them. I remember spending a lot of time trying to protect Fizz and the big twins from the chaos. I couldn't explain to them that Dad had had a bit too much to drink, and that he didn't act right when he did, and I spent a lot of my early years feeling angry at his choices. We'd see glimpses of his good side but he would let us down again and again. So many family events were ruined because of Dad's disease, and when he ultimately moved out, we didn't see him that much. He'd rented a small flat nearby to stay close, but his drinking spiralled after the divorce, and naturally losing his family was a traumatic thing for him to go through. Mum and Dad remained amicable because of us kids, but I know the split was difficult for them – it rocked the whole family to the core.

Our father-daughter relationship kind of disappeared for quite a few years as he struggled with his own stuff, and I spent a lot of time after the divorce dealing with a lot of anger. But the older I got, and the more his addiction escalated, the more I started to understand that he wasn't in control of his situation. And when I was able to comprehend what he was dealing with, I could support him more. I could've easily turned my back on him, but he was my dad, and my instinct was to help, so our relationship flipped, in that I was now trying to take care of him rather than the other way around. In some ways, there's a beauty in that, but there's also pain, because it shouldn't be that way around. However, now that I've had a child, I understand that parent-child relationships aren't always straightforward. We grow up and think that our parents should be completely focused on us, and that everything should be about their children, and in many ways it should. But we forget that our parents are human, and that they're also still growing up and maturing, or trying to understand themselves, or just going through things that we might never understand.

My dad has spoken about his upbringing being the thing that triggered a lot of his issues. He didn't have as much love as he needed growing up, and I'm sure that impacted who he was as an adult. As a mum myself, I'm constantly trying to be my best for Lucky, and I realise I didn't know myself the way I thought I did before I had him. It's easy and normal to get angry or disappointed when we witness our parents not being 100% or letting us down, but now I'm a parent, I realise that we grow with our children, and that the self-development never stops.

My dad's journey in overcoming his addiction wasn't easy. It took him many years, and Mum's passing, for him to finally go to rehab and get himself clean. I used to have nightmares he'd relapse, because I was so scared to lose him again and I knew how quickly the addiction could take over.

Dad has come to a place where he's healthy and sober, and has been for many years now, which I'm so happy and proud about. I'm more proud because he's been really open and honest with us about his journey. He still has cravings most days (they never go away) but he's still fighting hard. The whole family has been so proud of him these past five years, and the two of us have developed a strong relationship again, when it didn't always feel possible. Now that he's come off the drink, it's almost like he's a completely different person. That's actually been quite a shock, because I didn't realise addiction could change a person so fully.

I'm able to see more of his true personality now that he's sober, which is nice, gentle and loving. We've grown so close since I've had Lucky, too, and the love Dad has for him has made me respect him even more.

CHAPTER TWO

We were just a normal family until Louis went to an *X Factor* audition when he was 18. After that, everything changed. That was it – he was gone and he never came home.

We were all there to support him during his first audition, as a solo artist in the boys category, and it was exciting to meet the presenter, Dermot O'Leary, who we all thought was amazing. *The X Factor* was such a big show back then, and we were huge fans, so it felt crazy watching Louis compete.

Of course we believed in him, but we also knew how big the competition was and managed our expectations. We just thought it'd be a nice experience for him and that maybe he'd get through to bootcamp, but it probably wouldn't go any further than that. And when he didn't make it past the final stage of bootcamp, we were gutted but realistic, and thought we'd just go back to normal life.

Then one day, Mum called us at the house to say that Louis had been put in a boy band. We thought it was a joke. We genuinely thought she was winding us up. But Simon Cowell was mentoring a group of boys for the 'Judges' Houses' category, and Mum sent us a picture of Louis, Harry, Niall, Zayn and Liam on a flight of steps. I was speechless. Even after they made it through to the live shows, we kind of thought Louis' good luck was going to end any minute – it just wasn't what happened to normal people like us, was it?

Our family was given a set number of tickets to attend the performances, so we used to alternate, and I remember dressing up in this full maxi dress and head-band to watch Louis. To us young kids, it honestly felt like we were going to the Oscars. When his group made it to the finals, we were so proud of them, and when they finished third, we were all crying our eyes out.

Even so, we thought it was over for them, before all of a sudden the boys were travelling to Los Angeles! Never in our wildest dreams did we think any of us would be travelling to LA. The whole process was a whirlwind, the start of all our lives changing.

It was obviously Louis' dream to do music, but there's no way he could've prepared for how quickly things developed. He was an 18-year-old lad, and the whole experience was like buying a lottery ticket and not really thinking you're going to win. But Louis did win the lottery, and it took some adjusting, not just for him but for all of us.

It was hard for Mum especially because Louis was her golden boy, her first born, and they were like best friends. I've realised exactly how hard this must've been since I've become a mum. If Lucky left home at 18, I can't even imagine how I'd feel. And not just to go to university, but to travel the world and do these crazy exciting things.

You can't help but worry about your children, however old they are. And even though Mum had encouraged Louis to audition, none of us were prepared for how big he would get. For me, it was mental coming home from school and seeing our front garden full of girls and press waiting to get to him. Once Louis entered the limelight, there seemed to always be people outside our door. I don't even know how they found out where we lived. Some of the filming for *The X Factor* took place at the house, so I guess that's how – and I'm a bit wiser now about how the press work!

In general, though, we were absolutely buzzing about the journey we were on with him, which started as a small theatre tour of the UK, and we loved going to watch and support the band. We often met the other boys and their families, too, and celebrated together during after-show parties. We all became a little unit and a lovely support system for each other.

Louis finding stardom through *The X Factor* wasn't the only dramatic change in our family. About a year or so after my parents split, Mum met her second partner, Dan, so we were going through quite the transitional phase all around. It was strange and confusing for us kids to see Mum with someone else after Dad, as any of my readers who have stepparents will know. When you only ever see your mum with your dad, it's then hard (and pretty weird) to see her with someone else. It's quite a confusing time for young children to go through their parents' divorce and then adjust to a new person coming into the family. When I think back on it now, I'm sure it was hard for Mum to navigate as a parent, especially deciding how and when to introduce her new partner to us. Before the big reveal, we could feel something had changed in her, that there was a kind of secrecy we weren't used to. Now, as an adult, I understand that her priority was to try and establish the relationship with him first, and to make sure it was going somewhere before she introduced him to us.

Meanwhile, amongst all the change, I was still struggling at school. By the time I was 15, I was still hoping to enter sixth form (for all the wrong reasons, like the fact I'd be ditching my school uniform and wearing my own clothes), but I'd taken my GCSE exams and failed to get the six Bs I needed. I was absolutely devastated. My whole school life I'd dreamt of being able to decide my own outfits and wear a little makeup, and I assumed I'd move on to sixth form and be all grown up like the rest of my mates. Instead, I was left wondering what the hell I was going to do next. Mum could've appealed the decision, and I pleaded with her to do it. But straightaway she knew that school wasn't necessarily the right place for me and asked me what I wanted to do instead.

A year before, during the school holidays, I'd done some work experience with One Direction's hair and makeup artist Lou Teasdale, someone I now consider part of my inner circle of friends. We'd met a few times before the tour as she'd been doing the boys' hair and makeup on *The X Factor* even before the band took off; I'd see her around while supporting Louis during his TV performances. It was during Year 10 when Mum initially arranged for me to do some work experience with Lou's agency, The Book, which she ran with her twin sister, Sam.

I went down to London for a few weeks to work in their offices and see how the agency looked after their hairdressers, makeup artists and photographers, but I didn't enjoy it. My shyness just got in the way. But because Lou's career was blowing up – not just because of the boys' success, but also because she was working on a DIY beauty book – she asked me to be her assistant on a shoot for a couple of days. Lou still remembers me being frightened and scared to death, which they all wag me about now. I just wouldn't speak. But even though Lou felt sorry for me, she saw me as out of my depth. She's since said she thought I should be doing some 'normal' work experience up north instead. It's mental how different things have turned out to be!

After learning about my grades, Mum said to me, 'If you want to do beauty, you can go and assist your brother's makeup artist on tour, because that's the best experience you're gonna get.' In Mum's mind, being able to put on my CV that I assisted the hair and makeup artist on One Direction's tour would open so many doors for me. And I would only have to go down for a week of work experience. But I hadn't enjoyed my time at The Book the year before, and I couldn't wrap my head around flying out to America on my own and being on tour with the boys. What did that even entail? I was so shy, and never liked leaving my family, even on holidays, so I told her no.

'I can't … I can't!' I cried.

'You're going!' Mum said.

'What?!'

We were driving in the car when she rang up Lou.

'Mum!' I cried, 'Nooo!'

'C'mon now, it's fine... ' When Lou picked up, Mum said, 'Lottie didn't get into sixth form, so she's gonna come and assist you for a week.' Basically, Mum told Lou exactly what was going to happen. She was that kind of person, someone who took opportunities where she could and wanted to make sure her children succeeded. I imagine she didn't want us living the way we grew up, happy but struggling to make ends meet, even though she worked incredibly hard.

Lou couldn't really say no as she worked for Louis, but in the end, it all worked out alright. Much later, Lou told me that she never even needed an assistant but was ultimately grateful to have some help for the week and beyond. And who knew then that we'd go on to be so close?

When Mum told Louis that I'd be coming on tour with him for a week, he probably wasn't over the moon. He was living out his rockstar dreams and probably hadn't envisioned his little sister being there with him. Then again, we thought it would only be for a week of work experience and then I'd come home.

Before my first international flight, I'd only been on a plane a handful of times, the first to visit a pen pal in Jersey when I was 12. And now I was 15 going on 16, and soon to be flying business class, it all felt so daunting. I remember Mum telling me that I would be getting a bed on the flight, and me not understanding what she was talking about.

'Your seat lays down into a bed,' she said.

'On the plane? Like how?'

'And you get a three-course meal...'

I was so shy and nervous that first week, but looking back, being thrown into the deep end was the best thing that could have happened. It was just the thing I needed to get myself out there.

Between assisting Lou with getting the boys ready and watching the shows, I'd have a bit of fun in New York City. And once I'd got over my nerves, and realised what an adventure I was on, I decided it was a no brainer for me to stay. To be honest, what other choice did I have? Did I really want to go back to the UK, where I'd feel sorry for myself and try to figure out what was next?

Instead of staying for a week, I ended up travelling for two years between 2013 and 2015, across the United States, South America, Asia, Australia and Europe as One Direction performed their Take Me Home, Where We Are, and On the Road Again tours. Never in my life did I think I'd be doing anything like that, but as exciting as it was, it was also just nice to be around my brother, because I wouldn't have been seeing much of him back home.

At the time, I didn't really understand that this was a once in a lifetime opportunity for a working-class

16-year-old girl from Doncaster, and I will forever be grateful that Mum had the foresight to set me off on that journey. As a mum now myself, I hope to do the same for Lucky. I want my son to know that his passions and dreams are possible to achieve, whatever those will be.

Assisting Lou gave me an insider's look into the world of being a hair and makeup artist. I was no longer sat at home watching YouTube videos but assisting an artist in a busy work environment surrounded by loads of people and involving loads of pressure.

It was also interesting to learn how other people entered this world. Lou had moved to London at 18 and graduated from the London College of Fashion. She assisted for barely any money before moving on to *The X Factor* as part of their big hair and makeup teams. Every year she'd tour with different acts from the show, watching bands and personalities get signed up, have their big moment, then fall away. But One Direction kept growing and growing, and Lou ended up sticking with them permanently and leaving the show.

Lou had experience working during London Fashion Week, where she'd do the makeup of 20 guys for a runway show. She'd also done makeup for music videos, so had a very good understanding of putting makeup on boys. Part of my learning was watching her do very natural looks on Louis, Harry, Niall, Zayn and Liam. As Lou puts it, 'They wanted to look fit but didn't want to sit in a chair for ages.' The boys obviously had stressful schedules. They'd be tired or hungry or both, and just want to be in and out of the makeup chair. So Lou made them glow a bit and fixed their hair but didn't overdo it. 'They never want to look like their mum's dragged them down the salon and made them have a haircut,' she once said. 'They just want to look quite cool.' Lou understood that sometimes the biggest hairdressers in the world couldn't achieve or understand that kind of look, but she just clicked with the boys and knew what they needed.

I never really did the boys makeup, that was all Lou, and she was so good at it. My job was just to assist, and I enjoyed it. Seeing makeup from a different perspective was a huge learning curve for me, but I liked learning on the job, and it was like years of training packed into a few months. Anything Lou knew ultimately rubbed off on me, but something else I learned was that it wasn't enough to be able to do the talent's hair and makeup, there also had to be a level of social awareness. The boys just wanted to be comfortable and relaxed in their dressing rooms, so mindlessly chatting away with them wouldn't have been nice. It's funny, because Lou really got on well with the boys, who were all just normal lads so she could relate to them. But she still knew how to have boundaries. We had to be respectful of their space, and they needed to know that people wouldn't be filming them or listening to their private conversations or getting involved in their matters. Lou says that's not something that can be taught, and thankfully it was a skill that came naturally to me.

I'd been around the boys since the X Factor days, so I could already gauge that after a show, or even while they were getting ready, they'd need privacy and time for themselves. It's mad to think that even a skill as subtle as that proved to be useful in the work I was doing, but the small details are just as important as the bigger ones.

When someone's that famous, they're meeting new people every single second. And often, strangers feel they have the right to just go up and speak to them, forgetting that they've got fans doing it all day long. But because I'd been around the boys for quite a while already, I understood that they needed that time and space to be on their own.

*

When I joined the tour, Lou was 15 years older than me, so in some ways we were an unlikely match in terms of friendship, but we immediately clicked, which helped settle me into the tour more quickly. Lou was warm and bubbly, and it was comforting that she had a similar accent to me, both of us being from Yorkshire (me from Doncaster, her from Hull). We were both northern girls with nice, close-knit families, and Lou was a twin, another similarity because of the two sets of twins in mine.

As our relationship progressed, it became clear that we both had a strong work ethic; we were both hungry and passionate about making something of the opportunities that came our way. Lou had worked hard to get where she was, and it was crazy to be learning from her. My job as Lou's assistant was basically to make her life as easy as possible, and to be as helpful as possible. Every evening before the big shows, I'd unpack her makeup kit, lay out the products, pick out bits I knew she liked from her own makeup bag and put them in the kit. I'd make sure she had a Diet Coke and her phone charger and put everything she needed in the corridor so she could run off set without thinking. I'd also make sure the boys were in their hair and makeup chairs on time.

During the day, we'd be travelling to the next destination by bus or plane, and sometimes Lou and I would even get to take the private jet, if there was enough space to tag along with the boys. Then we'd get to the next hotel and have a bit of free time to sleep before heading to a new venue around 4pm, where we'd set up, have dinner and get everyone ready in plenty of time before the evening show at about 8:30pm. The fast pace of tour life could be tiring, but I was young and had the energy, and never once thought it was too much. It just felt exciting, a bit like being in a dream. I was flying on a private jet, staying in the most amazing hotels, and watching the boys perform. What wasn't to like?

We weren't just doing the hair and makeup for One Direction and their various support acts, including the Aussie band 5 Seconds of Summer, we were also doing it for anyone else who wanted it. We often put makeup on the boys' girlfriends, mums or sisters, even personal assistants, and these were times when Lou could teach me and I could practice on girls other than my sisters. Sometimes people on the crew might want a haircut, so we did that too. Lou and I would also post pictures of us on Snapchat – which was huge at the time – or film little tutorials. She was also doing stuff for a hair brand at the time, so she'd do content for them when we had a spare moment.

We'd stick around waiting for the quick change as the boys came on and off the stage, then we'd wrap up around 10pm and get on a convoy to the next location. At the end of every gig, One Direction would play this song called 'Act My Age', which was a bit like an Irish jig, and that was usually the cue for the boys to come off stage and run towards the convoy before the fans could get to them. A bunch of us would be running towards the vehicles and I'd be laughing and screaming and dancing on the way out.

There were so many people working on the tour – about 50 of us divided into groups – and we became one big family. 'A' party involved the talent and principles, including each of the boy's personal security, tour managers and band management, while 'B' party involved the creatives, including all the hair and makeup people, who travelled with 'A' party and stayed in the same hotels as them. 'C' party was the crew, the people who moved the stage and things like that, and there were probably about 40 buses of crew, so the whole thing was a huge operation but very well managed and organised. Louis has been living that life for years, but it will forever remain a crazy little part of my life and something I'll be forever grateful for.

Initially, Lou didn't think I'd stay for as long as I did – and neither did I! She told me much later that when Mum called her to say I was coming on tour for a week, she'd been quite stressed. Tour life was intense at the best of times, but she also had a young daughter with her part-time. Lux was only a baby, and while Lou was working and spending time with her daughter, she was also juggling a new relationship with one of the stage managers. In Lou's mind, all she was doing was five lads' hair – lads who only wanted to sit there for ten minutes anyway – but she still wanted to reassure my mum that she'd teach me what she could. So even though Lou said yes to me being there, the last thing she wanted was to feel like a babysitter for one of the talent's sisters. She also assumed I'd be a bit entitled and see the gig as more of a holiday. Lou had gone through a lot of assistants while working with the band, and none of them had stuck because while they liked the 'fun stuff', they weren't prepared to do the work. It wasn't all glitz and glam, and some people didn't appreciate that.

When Lou was starting out, she'd do the graft and grab every opportunity that presented itself, but when she was more established, she started coming across a different generation with a different attitude. These kids would ask her when they could leave, or say they wouldn't do certain stuff, which she'd never have dreamed of doing when she working her way up. In contrast, I often did things she never even asked me to do, which she appreciated. It's another reason Lou and I gelled right from the beginning.

I never took being on tour for granted and was happy to do any of the jobs, fun or not. That's just how real life works. It also made Lou want to invest in me more – she's always said to me that she saw a bit of her in me. We were both grafters, willing to do everything and anything we could. I could've easily gone on tour and not mucked in with the crew because I was Louis' little sister, but I wanted to be a normal member of staff, so I did everything the team did. That's ultimately why I ended up staying for two years. I saw the role as a job rather than an opportunity to tag along on my brother's tour, doing a bit here and a bit there. I genuinely wanted to get stuck in and to be a good assistant.

Just after joining the tour in 2013, Lou tried to school me on the proper way to act as part of the crew. But I didn't always listen to her at first and had to learn the hard way.

My first end-of-tour party (for Take Me Home) took place that November in Chiba, Japan. We had started off in London and after about 100 shows across Europe, North America, Australia, New Zealand and Asia, we were finally done and ready to celebrate. Lou had informed me that we didn't drink with the boys, and I was also only 16. However, I was determined to experience the nightlife just like everyone else and test the boundaries of my newfound freedom. So when Lou said to me, 'Do not come to me hammered. It's not professional, this isn't a party for us,' it went in one ear and out the other.

While Lou was catching up with her stage manager boyfriend who she hadn't seen for ages, I was being tempted by the big bowls of drink at the club. I'm sure someone nudged me to go on and have just one, and once I did, I was gone. I can't even remember how I ended up so drunk, but I was young, so a few drinks would've done me in. It wasn't long before people were telling Lou that I was being sick in the bathroom, and I do remember Lou coming in and telling me off. 'I told you not to do this!' she said. 'It's not my problem!' She had no sympathy for me because as far as she was concerned, it was my own fault, and I had to suffer the consequences.

My head was in the toilet the entire night. 'I'm sorry, Lou, I'm sorry,' I kept grumbling, between throwing up and speaking to my new boyfriend, Tommy, back home on FaceTime. Eventually, one of the security guys took pity on me and took me back to the hotel, and my tail was stuck firmly between my legs for the next few days. I got in a bit of trouble for that, but it was a good eye opener for me and a reminder of how seriously I had to take things. I never did it again.

Lou was like a big sister, mother and best friend rolled into one. I spoke to my mum constantly on tour, mainly on text because of the time difference, squeezing in phone calls when I could. But Mum couldn't physically be there, so Lou's guidance and friendship was a huge comfort.

We'd have our own hotel rooms booked for us, but we always ended up staying in each other's rooms and having sleepovers. We'd spend the night mainly gossiping, and since then we've been a massive support to each other through all kinds of stuff. At the time, she was on and off single, while I was figuring out my own love life. I'd met my first boyfriend when I was 13 and it was very much a school kind of relationship that lasted for a couple of years. But even though that relationship had ended by the time I joined the tour, I was still feeling up and down over him – typical teen angst. I had met my new boyfriend Tommy halfway through the tour, and Lou would listen to me if I was upset about something and give me advice, and I'd try to do the same with her.

My memory's a bit all over the place because of the grief I've suffered since, but Lou remembers a night in New York when I was going through the worst period pains. I was writhing around in bed, crying my eyes out, and Lou eventually said, 'Right, I'll go,' before marching out of our hotel at 3am in the pitch black (not really advisable in New York) and looking for painkillers. We could've never asked a tour manager to do something like that for us, but we could do those things for each other.

I'd sometimes act as Lux's babysitter, or Harry's sister Gemma would take her out as a chaperone. Lux didn't fully tour with us, but her father would fly her out as much as he could so Lux could be on tour with Lou. It was very hard for Lou not having her daughter around full-time, but for Lou it was a case of providing and creating a life for her daughter. Looking back now as a mum, I don't know how Lou did it, but I can see how much strength and courage she had to have to be away from her baby. I'm lucky to be in a situation now where I can build my career and earn money while still pretty much being a full-time mum with Lucky, so I can't imagine having to be away from him like that and the toll it must take.

When we did have Lux on tour with us, the boys loved having her around and treated her like a little mascot. Louis in particular knew how to play with her properly because he'd grown up with so many babies and toddlers, as had I. I was buzzing to have a cute little three-year-old to look after when I had the time.

On days off, it was difficult for us to go out and enjoy ourselves because there were always One Direction fans around. They'd obviously come for the big concert, so we'd encounter mobs of them anywhere we went, and they'd follow us around wanting to chat and take photos. Sometimes we'd have fans staying in the same hotels as us. It was nice being able to meet young people from different places in the world, but we also needed our rest and privacy and having to interact all the time could be exhausting. That's why we spent so much time watching *The Only Way is Essex* in our room, despite being in the most amazing cities in the world. It was just too stressful to do much else.

There was something nice about having Lou as a friend rather than a boss. She could tell I was hungry to do well, and that I was passionate about beauty, and it made her want to help me succeed. The tour taught me so much, not necessarily about applying makeup – that was a small part of it – but about myself and who I could be one day. The opportunity was the first step towards finding my own confidence, whereas before I couldn't even interact properly with people.

From travelling, to learning how to work with others, to the craft of applying makeup, it all gave me a sense of self-worth, and the extra time I was given on tour made me feel like I was doing something right. And meeting new people every day taught me how to have proper conversations. My relationship with Louis also changed and grew deeper. At first, it was probably annoying having his little sister on tour, but he agreed for me to stay, and we quickly appreciated how special our set-up was. He had probably assumed that being on tour wouldn't allow him to see much of the family, while I thought I wouldn't see much of him at all. Those times we shared created the bond that we have now, as I'm the only person in the family who can relate to the crazy things he went through. We were a comfort to each other, and although we were far from home, we never felt homesick. Now, Louis and I talk about those times being the best of our lives because it was just before everything changed.

Wherever we went, crowds of fans would wait

outside our hotels, or the venues the boys were playing at, and while they were obviously excited to see Louis, they were excited to see me as well, having seen me around on the tour.

That recognition was cool, but it also had its downsides. One day, a fan took a candid photo of me as we were headed from a hotel to a waiting car. And when I saw that photo, sometime at the beginning of the tour, my first thought was, *I don't like how I look there … I'm carrying a bit too much weight.* It was the first time I became aware of what it was like to be in the public eye. No one had ever been critical about how I looked, but I still wanted to feel better about myself and my body image.

It was easy to overindulge on tour, what with everything being on tap, but I became more aware of what I was eating and made better food choices. I'd never worked out before at all but started to do some exercise. I was more grown up now and starting to become a lot more self-aware. If Lou and I weren't bingeing boxsets at the hotel for a bit of downtime, then we were at the gym. It wasn't a drastic body transformation, but it made all the difference in terms of my insecurities and started me on my journey.

CHAPTER THREE

For each leg of the tour, we'd have a month of being abroad, end with a wild end-of-tour party, then take a week off to spend at home with our families.

It was during one of those weeks that I'd met my boyfriend, Tommy in Scunthorpe and entered into the first mature relationship I'd ever been in. But we hardly got to spend any time with each other in the beginning, and every time I came home to Doncaster, I found myself having a taste of home life again, then struggling to leave for the next leg of the tour (I didn't just miss being at home or with Tommy when I was on tour, I also missed English food. I know it sounds silly, but I craved simple stuff like beans on toast or a good cup of tea. You couldn't get those things abroad, or at least not how it was back home).

After Louis rose to stardom, the whole family moved into a new house in a friendly and quiet village called Gringley on the Hill. Beacon House was bought while I was touring, and the most exciting part about coming home was no longer sharing a room with my sisters. Fizz and I had the top two bedrooms in the loft conversion, and as young girls who had never had their own rooms before, we were absolutely buzzing.

Now that we were all a bit older, our personalities were developing more. While Phoebe and Daisy would see me as the protective sister who always took the sensible approach, they saw Fizz as the older sister they could go to if they simply wanted a 'yes'. Fizz was the sister who didn't take anything that seriously, but also the sister who spent time upstairs on her own, while the rest of the family were downstairs.

Phoebe, Daisy and I were always into all the makeup and glam, but Fizz had other interests and different views to the rest of the family, which she'd often voice at the dinner table if someone said something she didn't agree with.

We'd not only moved into a new house, which took some getting used to, but in the summer of 2014, Mum also remarried. Mum and Dan seemed happy, and we were glad that Mum was experiencing a nice, normal relationship and a bit of stability.

She'd planned her wedding so that all of us – me, Louis

and all the One Direction Boys – could be there during a moment when we weren't touring. On her wedding day, Mum wanted me to do her makeup and it felt like such an honour. I didn't think of myself as a makeup artist at that stage, but she trusted me enough on her big day to make her look perfect. It's such a special memory for me, and I still remember her sitting there all relaxed as I did her makeup – making sure to take special care to make her feel as beautiful as possible – with the wedding photographer taking pictures in the background (these days, it's become normal for everyone to come to me to have their makeup done – even Nan asks sometimes when we're going out for some family event!).

We also had two new additions to our family – the little twins, Doris and Ernie, who Mum had with Dan in 2014.

Phoebe and Daisy were buzzing because it was their turn to have one baby each to look after, effectively becoming little mums themselves at the age of 10. Mum trusted the big twins to look after the little twins, and Doris and Ernie have always been a special part of our family.

Before having them, Mum had longed for more children, but had struggled to conceive. We'd all been on the journey with her from every failed IVF attempt through to pregnancy. At every stage we were so nervous for her, but when she got to three months and the bump came, we were hopeful for success. When Doris and Ernie were born, they seemed like little golden miracles to us. And each time I came home to visit, they'd be so much bigger, as the tour was right at the start of their little lives.

The big twins and the little twins spent more time in Beacon House than I did, and for them it was a home filled with antiques, because Mum had come into a new phase of her life where she was obsessed with all things traditional.

The names Doris and Ernie were quite old-fashioned, and when she first mentioned them to us, we begged her not to use them. 'You can't name them that!' Now, we adore their names, which suit them so well, but at the time they felt quite unusual. , I remember saying, 'How are we gonna tell people that our sister is called *Doris*?' Then again, people said the same thing about Lucky's name. Loads of people, including Nan, said, 'You can't call him *Lucky*!' But I just thought, *Well, he's our child, we can call him what we want.* And children grow into their names.

So, Doris and Ernie had these names that felt different to ours, the house was filled with old furniture, and parcels being delivered to the house everyday, most of them either more old furniture for the house or baby outfits for Doris and Ernie, who Mum loved dressing in little frilled outfits like they were royals.

Mum had never been bothered about interiors before, probably because she couldn't afford to think about stuff like that. But Louis loved our mum so much and was so generous with her. He'd given Mum her dream home, so she spent her time doing it up exactly as she wanted, falling in love with décor and online shopping. She deserved it too – she'd done so much for us growing up, so it was amazing to see her enjoy herself.

She also loved learning new things, and when Daisy and Phoebe started having horse-riding lessons down the road from the new house, a few weeks later Mum decided to join them in a class. The big twins were a bit shocked, but the three of them ended up riding together with Dan watching on. It was a really special time of our lives.

Though Mum was encouraging and determined, and still working incredibly hard, she was still so soft in those days. On the off chance that Daisy or Phoebe didn't feel like going to school, she wouldn't really argue or even try to persuade them.

We have a lot of cherished memories of Mum back then that we talk about often, like the fact that she had a reputation for being late: if she said a time, you always had to add 10 to 20 minutes onto that. As Daisy puts it, 'Mum was good at doing a million things at once, organising everyone else's life instead of her own.' She was a bit messy, a bit chaotic, but in a sweet and charming way. She had so many kids to juggle alongside her midwifery work, so it all made sense. And whenever we all went out, she'd seek out a table with a baby to fuss over. In fact, she was friendly and open-minded with everyone she met.

Coming back home to Mum, the rest of my family and Tommy was always bittersweet. I never wanted to leave so soon, and always thought I needed an extra few days. But the one time I called Lou and told her, I was a bit shocked at her reply: 'You're either working on this tour, or you aren't.' Looking back, I was too young to understand the opportunity that had been given to me, and Lou knew first hand that everyone involved had to be committed. She didn't want to be hard on me but that was the lesson I needed to learn. Every person on that crew had to do every single day or nothing at all.

Lou had had to juggle and sacrifice so much to be there herself and knew she'd been lucky to negotiate a deal that allowed her to travel with the boys while having Lux. That the band were willing to accommodate Lou and her baby was because they felt comfortable with her and trusted her. Lou even remembers Louis having conversations with management alongside her while she explained how she'd be able to work with her new baby. It wasn't just One Direction's image that was important to them, it was also who they had around them. The job was a huge commitment, and she knew that the boys wanted people who would work as hard as they did, while feeling like family.

Lou also wanted me to know that Louis was doing all of this for me, and for my family. Therefore, I had to learn the tough way that I couldn't act as I pleased when part of a team. I had goals and ambitions, and I wanted to do big things and progress in my career. I couldn't throw these things away because of a new relationship. I had to get on with it, show that I wanted to put my all in and respect the vibe the crew had created.

Of course, Lou also knew how hard it was to be away from a new relationship, and for our next week off, we organised a holiday in Tulum, Mexico. Tommy came out to meet us and I felt happier with it all. From time to time, Mum would visit, too, which Louis and I loved, because we missed her so much, and we knew she missed us, too.

For my 17th birthday, Mum flew out to New York and threw me a big party on the rooftop of the Jane Hotel. I thought that was the coolest thing ever, a party just for me in New York City. We all had an amazing night, and it was nice that Mum could see what she'd created. I'd found a bit more confidence as the tour went on and was no longer that shy and nervous girl who'd been reluctant to go on tour even for a week; instead I was a mature young woman travelling the world as part of a major team, working hard, and experiencing a whole new side to life. If I had felt useless and thick at school, being on tour made me feel capable and sure of my place. It also showed me that my dreams could come true.

*

One Direction had their last and final show of the On the Road Again tour in Sheffield on the 31st October 2015. I remember that night quite clearly because we were all crying our eyes out.

We couldn't believe they were done and that the adventure we'd been on was over. We'd been this big, supportive family, and now we all had to go our separate ways. While the boys went on hiatus to focus on their individual careers, and tour life came to an end for me after two amazing years, I decided to spend my time between Doncaster and London, renting a room from Lou in Hackney, East London. I also signed on to her agency, The Book, and we continued working together, but now it was more of a collaboration than a mentorship.

Even though I'd learned a lot from Lou on tour and gained a bit of belief in myself, I wouldn't say I'd achieved *peak* confidence, which isn't something that happens instantly or perhaps ever, at least not 100%. There are still things that I work on confidence-wise, despite considering myself quite at ease with myself in many areas of my life. Public speaking is one thing I'm still not comfortable with. It makes me so nervous!

I'd laid down some groundwork, but I still had a lot to figure out. Now that I was signed up with Lou's agency, I was required to go to meetings and jobs, but I still felt nervous to do so. On tour I was looked after. I had stuff booked for me and an itinerary to follow. Essentially, I was existing in a cosy bubble. I knew my role and my place within the system. I could turn up to set wearing whatever I wanted and just be behind the scenes. But now I was out in the real world, and all of a sudden it was just ME.

I was the person going to jobs and having to be in front of a camera. This was the beginning of me as a 'brand', even though I never thought about it like that, and it would take me a while to be comfortable with that fact.

I now had to learn a different set of skills to what I gained on tour. While Lou had taught me about the overall makeup industry outside of tour life, and how to act and how to be helpful, I had taught her how social media worked, showing her the latest trends. My childhood obsession with researching makeup brands, their products and learning from YouTube came in useful when I'd tell her, for example, that everyone was using a specific highlighter shade, and she'd get on board with that. And by 2016, she could see that the hair and makeup industry was changing, that it was slowly moving away from working in fashion – where you focused on face-to-face interactions with people, such as shooting with photographers and assisting the right people – to online content and brand partnerships.

The fashion world was quite rigid at the time, with people thinking of social media as cheap and not worth their time. But because I was with Lou all the time, she started paying attention, and while we had spent a lot of our free time gossiping about what happened on tour, or talking about lads, I was showing her content she never would've looked at otherwise, like those YouTube makeup tutorials. Most hair and makeup artists were ignoring the platforms, but Lou found it all amazing. She never claimed to know better than me because she was older, and I know that for her it was important to listen to and learn from the younger generation.

Early on she started speaking to brands and telling them what was happening. Lou's agency had taken a chance on me as 'an influencer', although it wasn't called that back then. It was a new way of representing a client, but Lou and I were giving each other so many valuable tools that and it felt like a match made in heaven. Straightaway, we both knew that we needed and could support each other. Lou continued showing me how to work my way up in the makeup world, anything from assisting makeup artists and making contact sheets to working at London Fashion Week, and she continued to teach me the importance of little things like being polite, friendly and on time, stuff that's second nature to me now. Even today when I'm timekeeping in my head, I think about how Lou taught me that. If I'd gone to sixth form, I might've missed out on those skills, like politeness and professionalism, all stuff instilled in me from ten years ago.

Instagram had officially launched in 2010, so some years later, Lou and I had gained quite a few Instagram followers since being on tour, mainly One Direction fans who all wanted that behind-the-scenes glimpse of what was going on.

You'll all probably know how huge the band's fan-base was, and that their fans were obsessed with the boys and anyone associated with them. So we wondered what to do with that audience and how to make it work for us. I'd started my own Instagram account when I was only twelve, before I was even doing anything worth promoting. In those early days, I was posting day-to-day stuff like selfies, photos of family and friends, pictures of my meals. I even remember posting a photo of an ice lolly, which makes me cringe. But by the time I joined the tour, and especially after, Instagram had established itself as a place where brands were paying people to create content. That's when Lou and I started thinking about our posts a bit more carefully and tailoring our feeds.

We were learning that if we wanted to work with a hair or makeup brand, we needed to be posting nice hair or makeup content and tagging the right companies – not just keeping a diary of, for example, being at work or with friends, even if it was relatable. It took me quite a while to get used to posting more professional content instead of posting whatever sprang to mind, but I realised over time that if I wanted to work with brands, I needed to be conscious of my content.

The first time Lou suggested I film a makeup tutorial for YouTube, I was embarrassed and nervous about it. I'd spent a lot of time watching those types of videos online but I never once thought I'd be good enough to do one myself. We'd become comfortable taking pictures and posting them, but she wanted me to start filming stuff.

'You're doing a tutorial,' she said. And when I protested, Lou added, 'We're doing one! We'll delete it after if you don't like it.'

Filming myself now and posting it online is second nature to me, but back then it was such a foreign concept to sit in front of a camera and film myself doing stuff. I was so worried that my friends would make fun of me, and I could even hear them saying, 'Who the hell does she think she is?'

I was mainly worried about how I'd look in the video. I was still so insecure, and it felt like such a big thing putting myself in front of a camera and seeing myself in HD. I knew there'd be little things I was still self-conscious about. Now, if someone wants to make fun of something I post, it won't worry me, but back then the thought made me so nervous. But I trusted Lou's instincts – after all, she *was* representing me. We knew people were making more and more makeup videos and using the brands they wanted to work with as a way of getting their attention, so she didn't see why I couldn't do it.

I remember we filmed a blue eyeliner look in the agency office, and after we shot the content and liked it, we were then trying to figure out how to edit it and make it all flow. What's funny is that now I'll get in front of my phone, film a video, chop everything together nicely, and put it up, easy as that. But it was all so alien back then, and it's mental looking back on how much of a learning curve we went on.

On tour, Lou and I couldn't be creative with our looks for the boys, but now we were able to play a bit more and experiment, posting photos of our creations, like the pink glitter lips look we once did. That video is still up on YouTube and you can watch me, step by step, as I apply Maybelline's Magnetic Magenta lipstick, add on a fixing spray, and use a brush to apply large chunks of sparkly Topshop glitter in periwinkle – so much fun!

The makeup trends coming out of sites like Tumblr were dramatic, stuff I'd not done before as I was still just getting to grips with the basics. But to get more makeup jobs, I filmed short makeup tutorials on Instagram and longer demos on YouTube. The quality of those videos when I look back are terrible, but it was a start. And even then I had an awareness of how important it was to move with the trends, paying attention to what was getting recognised. I'd constantly be scrolling on Tumblr, which was so big in those days, to see what was being posted and what was cool. Facebook had already been around since 2004, and there was something so exciting about getting those friend requests back in the day, but it wasn't a place to promote makeup, not like YouTube which had come out a year later.

When the trend for colourful hair came on the scene around 2015, Lou's twin sister Sam (who co-owns Bleach London) asked me to be a hair model. We wanted to try and post a look that was different and thought about doing an all-over rainbow hair style, where we'd dye each section of hair a different colour. But when someone came up with the concept of dyeing the roots rainbow instead, we thought that was a cooler idea. So, they dyed my hair, and we posted the pic all over social media. *Teen Vogue* picked up the story straight away, and the trend blew up after that.

Rainbow roots made me stand out and gave me something bold and colourful to offer beauty brands, who offered me fun and quirky gigs to run with for a while. Also at that time, I was obsessed with and known for being platinum blonde – inspired by Lou, who had been bleach blonde during the One Direction tour. Back then, we were living in that silver hair era, where girls were overdoing silver shampoo on bleached hair, which meant that Lou and I were always in the salon or buying bleach to do our looks. And because my hair was already bleached, I dyed my hair all kinds of colours from frosty pink to green – you could say that I finally got to live out my sixth-form dream!

My first paid job through the agency was for Ghost Fragrances in 2016. Lou had friends who owned a digital agency, and they were trying to get social media for brands off the ground. She pitched me for the fragrance gig, and we got the deal. The thought of me semi-acting in that video still makes me cringe, and I'd be nervous to do something like that now just because I know for sure that I'm not an actress. But the fee for that job blew my mind at the time: £6,000. Maybe it sounds naïve, but I honestly thought I was rich, and that I'd never have to worry about money again (Lou says I must've spent the money four times in my head, then bought a house with it).

I'd never experienced money like that as I hadn't been paid while touring, so I was happy and willing to do anything the agency could offer me. The video is somewhere out there on the internet, but the brand had me rehearsing a few lines and filming in a funky, neon-coloured science lab (mixing ingredients for a new perfume to help me attract my dream crush), and when the video starts, I'm on a dating app, swiping right with pink acrylic nails, repeating, 'No ... no ... no ...', before looking at the camera and saying, 'Sometimes it feels like every guy I meet is a total recipe for disaster.' I drop the phone into a little white cauldron and add my ingredients to make the Girl Crush fragrance.

That video is like a time capsule, a whole different chapter of my life. And even though it's all a bit embarrassing, it opened many doors for me. Since then, I'd actively steered away from roles like that. It shocks me that I ever had the courage to do it, and I can safely say that acting isn't one of my strong suits. But just starting out, I was up for doing anything and didn't want to disappoint.

As the branding jobs continued coming in, and my followers on social media grew, showing me that people did want to see my content and liked what they saw, the idea of hustling as a freelance makeup artist didn't seem as appealing anymore. Neither did waking up at 5am to assist makeup artists at London Fashion Week.

Don't get me wrong, I loved putting makeup on the models, but the power of what I could do with social media completely took over. I could express my creativity through makeup videos, apply the products that brands were giving me, and post about them online – never in my wildest dreams did I think I could make a name for myself this way or even make so much money from it.

By this time, brands like Nails Inc wanted to collaborate with me, which I couldn't quite believe. This was my biggest collaboration to date, and we planned to launch it towards the end of 2016. Nails Inc had decided to delve into makeup, and after a few meetings, we decided to do a range of nail polishes together with my own 'Lottie Lip Paints'. I'd be able to choose and name the colours and design the catchy packaging, which was so exciting.

We released a limited-edition set called 'Matchbox' and created four colour palettes: Rascal/Hell, Babes/Mint, Sick/Salt and Out Out/Buzzin. The partnership was a success, and so were the products, but there were lessons I needed to learn when it came to collaborations and business. Creating my own products and having my name on them was amazing, but looking back, I can see how much I wanted to people please. I thought I had to go along with what was presented to me because

I'd landed an epic deal with an established brand. But I was also saying yes to colours and packaging I wasn't fully happy with because I didn't want to go into meetings calling the shots and expressing my opinions.

The range wasn't completely to my taste, and I couldn't promote it how I wanted, and it showed me that if a partnership wasn't authentic to me, then it wasn't going to work. It wasn't about being unpleasant, it was simply about expressing my true feelings. If a brand showed me a colour I didn't like, I'd tell them. These were the sort of skills that would come in useful when I launched Tanologist a few years later.

I'd come a long way from dreaming of working on a makeup counter and desperately wanting to be a makeup artist. Now platforms like Instagram and YouTube were showing young creatives a different way to make a name for themselves and allowing them to gain the attention of big brands. And I'll always be grateful for social media because it provided a place for me to express myself and build the foundations of a successful business.

And I feel like apps like Instagram have evolved nicely since I started using it. Where before I used to whack any old thing up, now it's all very thought out. There's a lot more video content happening too, which is nice because it's more natural. Social media posts, especially on Instagram, have become an amazing way for people to promote themselves and brands, and it's given people the opportunity to start businesses when they probably thought they'd never be able to do so.

To fans and followers, it might look like not a lot of work goes into being an influencer, but there are so many things to consider if you want to be successful at it. When I first started out, deals with brands were so casual, you just used to get a job come in and get paid to do it. Now brands won't work with you unless your statistics stack up.

There weren't any stats on Instagram to begin with, so no one really had a clue about the breakdown of their followers. But now that stats exist for business and creator accounts, brands want to see an audience breakdown – they want to see the split between women and men, they want to see the age range of your followers, they want to see the location of your followers. If an influencer wanted to work with a UK brand for example, and they didn't have a high enough percentage of followers in the UK, they wouldn't be able to get the job. Right now, my audience feels really authentic to me: the majority of my followers are between 18 and 24 years old, which is quite young, and my male-female percentage split about 20-80, which is perfect, because most of the brands I work with around hair, makeup and beauty are aimed at women.

One of the biggest considerations for brands now is

something called 'link clicks'. They want to see that you have a high number of 'clicks', otherwise they won't book you. I struggled with the concept of link clicks for some time, especially with trying to work out how to make my posts engaging enough for people to want to click. It's definitely not all easy going! In fact, my work online can be obsessive because I have to pay very close attention to numbers and proving to brands that I can do what they want me to do. But this is the nature of any job – and being an influencer is a real job, whatever some people think. There's more that goes into the role than just putting on a bit of lipstick, posting a pic and getting paid loads of money. I've done this work for so long – I started from the very beginning – so I'm always having to adapt, experiment and learn, keep on top of the trends and move with the times.

It's true that the influencing world has become very saturated, but I don't necessarily see anything wrong with that. A lot of young girls message me saying they want to start a brand, and wanting to know what advice I can give, which is quite cute. And what I tell them over and over again is, 'Just be authentic. Be who you are. If you're going to do something, make sure you really believe in it, otherwise it just won't work.' Whether you're a Nano, Micro, Mid-tier, Macro or Mega influencer, every level has value and appeal, and I just want to help everyone.

Even though I've been influencing for so long, it's something I don't take for granted or ever get complacent about. When I go into a job, I still want to make the best impression, I still want to give them the best content. I make sure to understand what brands want from me, and that I'm able to fulfil that, and then I make sure to over-deliver. My goal is to leave a good impression on a brand so I can get more work from them and develop a good relationship. All these years later, I still make sure I'm polite and easy to work with, and that I'm always on time just as Lou taught me. The work I do is truly amazing, and I appreciate every trip or job that comes my way, just as I appreciate the money I make, the house I'm living in, and the amazing family I have.

As my career took off and I became more involved with the online world, the pressure to look 'perfect' continued to bother me.

I must've been only 17 when I first had my lips done. I knew I'd be modelling the lip products for the Nails Inc collaboration, and the whole thing made me really aware of my lips. I thought to myself, *I just need a bit of filler before I try and shoot this*, but regrettably I went to random people to do it because I was desperate to feel better about myself.

I used to have my lashes done at a particular place, and they had an aesthetic nurse come in once a week to do injectables. I thought it'd be the perfect thing to do, and once I had them, I remember feeling instantly happier because my lips were plumper. But when I looked at myself in the mirror, I could see that the woman hadn't done a proper job. I noticed there were lumps, and that one side was bigger than the other. After that, I spent a lot of time and a lot of money trying to correct the dodgy work this woman had done.

I used to go through a lot of pain getting them done (lip injections aren't nice), but in my mind it seemed worth it to build my confidence and look more like the women I was looking at online. My rush to feel better about myself had backfired, and because I was now so active on Instagram, the trolling began.

I've always considered myself relatively lucky when it comes to online abuse. It's such a horrible part of the world we live in and the job I do, but thankfully I've never been trolled that intensely. However, my fans and followers couldn't ignore what was happening with my lips as they grew bigger and bigger over the years. Even I had to agree with them after a while, because my fillers *were* getting out of control. It wasn't nice to hear, and personally I'd never dream of leaving a negative comment on someone's feed, but looking back they were probably right.

Once I started using filler for my lips, I went down this rabbit hole of focusing on the next piece of work, like having a sharper cheekbone (because I knew they offered cheek filler) or a sharper jawline (because they offered jaw filler). I always seemed to find something else to critique and 'make better', which had the potential to spiral out of control. I wished I'd given myself more time to let my face develop naturally, but it had become too easy to get swept up in looking at all these girls on Instagram and wanting to get work done to look like them.

On some level, even though I knew that women were enhancing and editing their pictures, using makeup, using fillers and all the rest of it, I still compared myself to them, and still wanted to look like them, and it became easier for me to go to any old person because I wanted it done quick or I wanted it done cheap.

I tried to hide the work as much as I could because when you get your lips done, it can be such subtle work – until it's not. I didn't speak openly about it, but of course I told my mum, who always remained gentle with me, telling me that I was beautiful the way I was and not to go overboard with it all.

Young women can grow their confidence through the various beauty products and procedures, but I do think it's important for people to do their research and find the proper people to do it, if that's the route they decide to take. The irony is that even though I explored all the treatments, I still wasn't satisfied with how I looked or how I felt in my body.

CHAPTER FOUR

By 18 years old, I never expected my passions to spiral into what they'd become. I took the opportunities that came my way and celebrated the wins with my family. The six or so months between the end of touring with One Direction and Mum falling ill are a bit of a grey area for me, but the overall feeling was one of enjoying home life again after two years away.

Nothing could really compare to being back home with my family again, seeing Mum, Fizz, the big twins, the little twins, Nan and Granddad, more regularly. I could finally enjoy Beacon House properly, too, and it was such a lovely house in comparison to the one we had grown up in. I dream of our old house in Bessacarr a lot, and have loads of fond memories of it, but Beacon House was obviously nicer.

I spent those six months travelling back and forth between Doncaster and London for work, but also reconnecting with friends from school. It was fun going to parties with them, and quite nice having people interested in what life had been like on tour and getting to share all my stories.

After travelling the world and being part of a unique family, I was readjusting to my old surroundings and what it was like to be a normal teenager again. But trying to socialise was a bit awkward. I'd lived a pretty crazy lifestyle for two years while my old classmates were going to school and focusing on their studies. Not many people could relate to what I'd been up to, which highlighted who I wanted to be friends with, who wanted to be friends with me, and who my real friends were.

It was nice being up north and young again, as opposed to working life, which at 15 going on 16 is quite a big thing. Even though being on tour wasn't your typical job, I saw it as a real job and took it very seriously. But while away, I'd missed out on all the normal stuff my peers were doing and now I was catching up and having a good time, taking part in little things like learning how to drive. So, when the news of Mum's illness hit me, I was thrown, once again, into having to be someone responsible and mature, dealing with something immense that most of my peers couldn't relate to.

Mum, who had helped me achieve my dreams when I thought myself a massive failure, was proud of me, and it was thanks to her that my life felt like a dream. About six months between ending the tour and building up my new career, my world soon turned into a nightmare. I'd been in London for a shoot around May 2016 and had gone back to Louis' house to stay that evening when Mum's partner Dan, rang me. As soon as he said, 'Mum's got leukaemia,' I broke down in tears.

Mum was in the background as he explained her diagnosis, but I don't think she could bring herself to talk to me and say the words. The idea of telling her children she had cancer must've been so horrific for her, and the reality probably hadn't sunk in for her yet. She'd been diagnosed with AML (Acute Myeloid Leukaemia), a severe form of blood and bone marrow cancer. I knew the two of them had just come back from Spain, where she'd been feeling poorly, complaining of being tired and run-down. She'd struggled to get out of the bed the whole holiday, but we all thought she was run down with really bad flu, we never guessed it to be cancer, even though she was getting progressively worse. When Mum and Dan came back to Gringley on the Hill, Mum noticed loads of bruising on her skin, so she went to see our family doctor.

By this point she seemed to be deteriorating quickly, and after the doctor took her bloods and the results came in, he sent her straight to University College Hospital London for treatment.

When Dan rang to tell me the news, it was such a shock and absolutely terrifying to hear because I never expected something like this to happen to our family. When other people talked about cancer, I naturally thought about how awful it was, but I never expected it to be something we'd deal with personally. I was in tears after the phone call and feeling scared by the weight of the news. Mum's condition was serious, so as soon as she knew, Dan rushed her down to London to try and get the best care, and he'd end up being by Mum's side the entire time, having a bed in the same room as her.

Right from day one, we were reassured that her condition was treatable. We were obviously very scared but held onto the hope that everything would be fine in the end. None of us ever expected this to happen to our mum, and it floored us and seemed so unfair. She was only 43 years old. She'd found a new lease of life, had fallen in love again, and then gone on to have two more beautiful children. She was living in the house of her dreams, and all her children were thriving, all thanks to her. We just couldn't understand how things could change so quickly.

Preparations were made for Nan and Granddad to move into Beacon House straight away to look after Phoebe and Daisy, and Doris and Ernie. My grandparents had just bought a retirement bungalow in the same village as us, about a 15-minute walk away. They were enjoying being nearer to us and would babysit when Mum travelled with Dan or went to see Louis. I decided that the best thing to do was move home permanently to help Nan out with the kids. At home, I took on the worry of trying to do everything I could to keep the rest of the family together. In that moment, Nan and I did what our instincts told us to do – it was less conscious and more primal.

Mum had been so nurturing, so loving and caring, and she had passed that onto me. It was also just a comfort to have Nan around. In many ways, she was what we had left of mum; they were so much alike, both loving and kind and hardworking.

While Mum and Dan were in hospital in London, Nan and I plodded along in Gringley on the Hill, trying to keep everyday life ticking by, feeding the kids, taking them to school, and entertaining them. Together we stepped into Mum's role to be there for the two sets of twins, and to try and keep their routines as normal as possible. We were all in a whirlwind but it also brought us together, as we wanted to be there for Mum and for each other.

I spent loads of time with Mum throughout her illness, taking any opportunity to be with her as much as I could. Our family spent time by her bedside, and there were days when she was better than others.

One of the hardest things to reckon with during Mum's illness was the shift in her person in a matter of weeks. We knew Mum as the centre of our world. She had all this strength and knew all the answers. Now she was laid up in a hospital bed, helpless. She didn't have the answers anymore, and her situation was out of everyone's control. As a family, we rallied together and thought, *Right, Mum's ill. She says she's gonna be okay, so she's gonna be okay. All we have to do is get through this. All we have to do is look after each other.*

From the start, we couldn't tell anyone about Mum's condition, not even close friends. I never knew why, exactly, but that's what she wanted, and we respected her wishes. Putting myself in her shoes, if I were ill, the last thing I'd want is everyone asking how I was all the time. My mum was the sort of person who didn't want people feeling sorry for her. She wanted to fight the cancer herself and with her family surrounding her. And I imagine she didn't want the news getting out to the public as well. But I found it quite hard and lonely not being able to tell anyone close to me.

For the first few months, Mum was still kind of herself, but it was obvious how scared she was between

It's been a hard road to get here, but I'm the happiest I've ever been. I can't believe how lucky I am to be living my life, and a mother to my beautiful boy.

My mum was the most beautiful
person – I love looking back at her
and my dad's wedding photos, and
when she was pregnant with me.

I miss her every day.

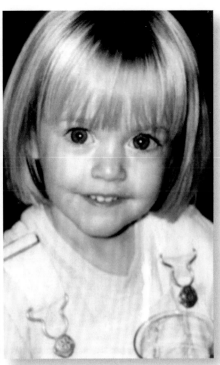

We didn't have a lot, but I loved my childhood in my noisy home surrounded by my brothers and sisters. Fizz and I always had a special bond and it's devastating to think that she's not with us. But I have the best memories and that gives me comfort now.

Mum always knew how much I loved makeup – it was amazing that she trusted me to do her's when she married Dan and it's one of my best memories of us together.

After my GCSEs I thought my life was over, but I had no idea that it was really just beginning. Being on tour with One Direction and meeting Lou was the best thing to happen for my career.

My early days in the business were so much fun – looking back at all I've done, I'm really proud of what I've achieved.

Meeting Lewis turned my world upside down, in all the best ways. He's my best friend and now we've had Lucky, I'm so grateful to have him by my side. He's an amazing dad and I can't wait for us to get married and grow our family.

I'm so lucky to have the support of my friends and family – Brits has been there for me through everything. My sisters, Phoebe and Daisy, are growing up and having families of their own now, and I love when we all get together. We've helped each other get through the hard years and are now looking forward to the future.

Our beautiful family.

the blood transfusions and the bone marrow transplants. Doctors would be coming in and out of her room as she received different bits of treatment. She'd lose her appetite a lot, so we'd try and encourage her to eat. Mum was in a private clinic which had a lovely chef called Ned, who she really liked, and he always made her whatever she fancied. He'd come into her room full of laughter wearing his chef's outfit, and his bubbly energy was nice to be around.

We tried to keep things as normal as possible, so Mum and I still talked about my work stuff. In between those hospital visits, I continued to throw myself into work because it was the biggest distraction that I could give myself, a way to take my mind off what was happening. Mum had pushed me to go after what I wanted, she had given me a leg up, so it made sense to keep establishing myself in the influencing world as other jobs came my way.

The agency and I were working with a publisher to create a makeup picture book. We called it *Lottie Tomlinson's Rainbow Roots #MAKEUPBYME*, but sadly Mum would never get to see that book. It had only been a short period of time that she was here to see my personal career take off, and when I think about that now, and how much I accomplished without her, or even because of her, it shows me how strong I've had to be throughout it all. But also makes me sad that I didn't have my number one supporter here to see it all unfold. I just know how proud she would've been of me.

Many months later, around October time, when Nails Inc were throwing a launch party for the Matchbox sets, Mum encouraged me to go and celebrate, but when I did, it was bittersweet, because I had wanted her to be there.

Mum's condition constantly worried me. We tried to do what we could to bring moments of joy to the situation, so when the hospital allowed her out for an evening, we all went to the theatre. Despite Mum having to leave early because she didn't feel well, it was so nice to go out and feel a bit normal again. For a while, Mum was allowed out of the hospital for daily visits to Louis' house in London, and for my 18th birthday, she managed to organise a celebration for the entire family even though she was poorly. She hired a tepee, the kind you see at festivals, which was set up in the garden, and we had a buffet-style picnic on the ground. My birthday cake was decorated with all sorts of edible cosmetics like lipsticks and eyeshadows. It was the last birthday I had with her, so the memory is bittersweet, but that was my mum all over, still making the effort to make us all feel special.

She was wearing a headscarf that day, because she'd lost all her beautiful cascading hair from the treatments. But Mum did manage to find a company that could make a wig out of her actual hair. We were so happy for her when it came because we knew how much it made her feel like herself again. It's hard for a woman to lose her hair because in many ways it's like losing an identity. But she experienced a nice pick-me-up with her new hair, and that gave Mum a bit of her confidence back.

As a family, we came together, trying to keep things positive and as normal as possible, especially for the big twins who were 12 and the little twins who were only two.

Because we were all in Doncaster at the time, I used to take the big twins and the little twins down to London to see Mum. We'd take the train and stay in a hotel around the corner, and Dan would come and help with the little ones whilst we were there. I have quite nice memories of all the twins in bed with Mum at the hospital, and we still very much treasure those photos.

None of us allowed ourselves to sit down and think about what could potentially happen. Even though we tried to keep the hope up right until the end, I felt a lot of hopelessness after seeing her in hospital because I knew there was nothing any of us could do. We kept saying she'd get better, but of course we knew how serious the diagnosis was. Having said that, for a long time we honestly never thought we would lose her. Even Nan never believed it to be possible.

When Mum went into hospital in London, a property had suddenly come up for sale in Gringley on the Hill, one they'd always admired and loved, called the Dovecot. It was closer to Beacon House than the bungalow and Mum suggested to Nan that she and Granddad go and view it. When Nan and Granddad did, they loved it. They sold their bungalow, bought the Dovecot, and throughout the whole exchange, Nan had hoped that Mum would come out of her illness and that once she did, she'd be closer to Beacon House to look after her daughter when she came home. It pleased Nan to have that belief because she never wanted to sit next to Mum in hospital thinking she was going to lose her – I knew it was what gave her strength.

Naturally, I was distraught about it all, and, not knowing what was going on, my friends used to ask if everything was okay. I pretended to be fine, but it must've been obvious to those close to me that something was wrong. I became more of a recluse, not going out as much, not at all myself. In the end, and for my own personal comfort, I confided in a few people that I trusted about the situation. You can't hide news like that for long.

Watching Mum slowly fade away was painful, and as the months went by, it was clear to see that we were losing her. It was hard for Mum to talk about what was happening, and she avoided those difficult conversations for as long as possible. It's like she didn't want to tempt death or admit to her children that she was dying.

After months of failed attempts at trying to get Mum better, the doctors at UCL told her there was nothing else they could do. When we found this out, I genuinely sat on the bathroom floor and cried, thinking there's no way I'd survive losing her. That was a turning point for us all. We suddenly had to face reality – we couldn't hide from it anymore.

Mum didn't want to pass away in London, so we all went home to Doncaster. The cancer had destroyed her immune system, so we had to be careful around her. Those of us who had colds or viruses had to stay away, while those of us who were healthy sat by her side. By that point, the disease had affected her so much and she couldn't speak that well, so we focused on just being together.

The nearest hospital to Gringley on the Hill was Sheffield Hospital about a half hour away. She went in and out for various bits, until she developed an infection and wasn't able to come home. We'd travel back and forth to see her, knowing that the end was near, and we just took it in turns to hold her hands and tell her that we loved her. One evening, after a visit, we all went home to get some sleep while Dan stayed with her in the night. The next morning, on the 7th December 2016, we were told that Mum had passed away.

It was only eight months between Mum's diagnosis and her passing, so most people were shocked to hear the news in the press. I was inundated with messages from friends, acquaintances and fans who all offered their condolences, and although the love and support from the public was heartfelt, it was difficult not having the privacy to deal with our emotions.

We held the funeral at Doncaster crematorium and kept the funeral small as Mum didn't want people she didn't know there. I've blocked most of that day from my memory, but two details stand out for me, one of them being much nicer than the other. Mum had requested we play 'The Luckiest' by Ben Folds at her funeral, and we did this as we walked out of the crematorium. It's something that's stuck with me because it shows so much about her character. Even in a time when Mum knew she was losing her life, she still considered herself lucky to have had us all. For her to have that attitude when she could've easily turned angry or bitter with the world, for leaving her children and losing her life at 43 says it all. It was such a sad day for all of us. We went to a local pub for her wake, and I drank so much to drown my sorrows and ended up throwing up at the end of the night. It was like I wanted to purge the day and the memory of it from my body.

Mum's funeral was just before Christmas, so when the day arrived it was hard for everyone. I can't remember her funeral one bit; it's probably another one of those moments I've blocked from my memory, but I do remember that on New Year's Eve, we set off floating lanterns in Mum's memory.

Christmas is one of those holidays that can feel particularly hard when you're grieving, especially if you've spent those weeks with that person every year. Not only are you dealing with the pain of their absence, but you're also dealing with all the festivities around you – the parties, everyone winding down for the year, the advertisements on social media, TV and in the shops, and everyone discussing their plans. Our first Christmas without Mum was unbearable especially because we lost her that December. Our emotions were fresh. They were raw and sad and difficult, and they looked different for everyone. And it was awful to think that we had more Christmases without Mum ahead of us. The holidays were supposed to be cosy, fun and celebratory, although I recognise it's not like that for everyone. Our family loved Christmas, and we were so used to spending it with Mum who was the one who went out of her way to organise something special.

As some of you know, I became an ambassador for Sue Ryder in 2020, during the Covid pandemic, and since then they've been such a helpful resource for me through my grief journey.

If you're someone who's currently grieving or has

lost someone in general and find the holidays hard, the charity has some pretty useful tips on how to deal with this time of year. It would've been nice to have gained access to this kind of online material after Mum's death. The charity suggests planning ahead and thinking about what you want to do on the day or during that December/ January period. Every person will be different, but it's important that you do what feels right for you. Because I come from a big family that I'm close to, I still wanted to share that time together, but other people might decide to spend that time with friends instead, or even spend it alone.

If you decide to spend it with a group of people, just remember that grief makes you feel one way one moment and another way the next, so don't be afraid to take some time for yourself, and don't be afraid to let people know how you're feeling every step of the way so that they're aware of what you need.

Sue Ryder also encourages people to think about starting new traditions of their own, if the old ones feel too triggering. If familiar traditions feel fine, of course stick to them, but just remember they can always change into something else. There are some lovely examples of stuff you can do on their website, like making your own ornaments in memory of the person who's passed, or even a paper chain with written memories on each link. Other lovely examples could be lighting a candle to remember a loved one by and using that time to think of them, or continuing to hang their stocking but having family and friends fill it with letters and cards. Dealing with grief can be painful enough and can take you on a rollercoaster of emotions even in one day. But what I've appreciated about my work with Sue Ryder were the tools I later learned after losing Mum and Fizz that still help me today.

The days, weeks and months after Mum passed away, none of us knew what to do with ourselves. With Mum gone, Nan and Granddad moved back home to the Dovecot, and Dan came back to Beacon House from the hospital, where all of us children stayed.

I prolonged my stay up north because everyone needed me – we were rudderless, everything was up in the air. Mum was gone, so the idea of having this career that I'd already started down in London didn't mean anything to me anymore. I lost hope. I wanted to give up on everything, but I couldn't give up on my family.

All of us were trying to come to terms with the fact that Mum was gone. I remember those times as hard and confusing, but we also had to keep things as normal as possible for Doris and Ernie, Phoebe and Daisy. I needed to be there to help with them and share the load. Even Phoebe and Daisy at twelve years old stepped up for the little twins and helped to look after them.

Mum and I had had some hard but meaningful chats

at her bedside before she passed. She'd told us all a wish she had, and that was to keep her memory alive for the little twins, so we've always worked hard to honour that. She never wanted them to forget her, so we've never stopped talking about her. Even today we feel such a big responsibility towards being the kind of influence she would've been for them. It's so unfair that Doris and Ernie never got enough of her, they never got what the rest of us experienced: that selflessness, that love and support, so we treasure them, and try to give them that little piece of Mum whenever we can.

Knowing that we needed to be there for the rest of the family and for the younger kids gave me a reason to live. Stepping into that mothering role after Mum passed away came naturally to me. Nan and I put all our focus into trying to maintain that same kind of daily routine that my mum would've had.

The big twins were old enough to sort themselves out in the mornings and catch the bus to school, but the little twins were early risers. They used to wake up around 6am, so we'd go and get them out of their cots and make them breakfast, bathe them, dress them, and play with them. They were such good kids.

While the little twins needed more practical support, the big twins needed more emotional support and guidance. Phoebe and Daisy needed something different from me after Mum's death; it's something we still talk about today. They wanted me to reassure them that I'd be a mum to them now; they needed me to step into that role, and it came instinctively.

Grief looked different for everyone, and although we didn't have the awareness to talk about our feelings back then, Daisy tells me now that when Mum died, she literally didn't believe it. When she heard the news, she spoke about Mum as if she were coming home the next day, which confused Phoebe, who completely understood that Mum was gone. But Phoebe never said anything to Daisy because she didn't want to upset her. At 12 years old, Daisy couldn't comprehend the news, and because she was in disbelief, her sadness took some time to come around, until after the funeral when it all started to get more real. What's mental is that Daisy had no recollection of any of this – it was Phoebe who told her what had happened. So that's what I mean when I say that grief affects your memory in so many ways. It's quite common for painful memories to be blocked out and to not remember a lot of what happened.

When there's children of that age going through grief, it's impossible for them to cope without a mother, and I wanted to give them the same love and guidance I'd received especially when it came to achieving their ambitions. As they grew up, I made it my priority to support whatever it was they wanted to do. The big twins wanted to follow in my footsteps, and I've helped to make that happen for them. I'm there to give them advice when they need it and to help them achieve whatever it is they want to do, and I'll keep doing that because I want them to continue to have that sense of my mum and what she did for me. I love being able to do that for them, it gives me so much joy to be that voice for them – and for my mum. I'm keeping the promise I made to her, and always will.

The twins were about 15 years old (around the same age I was when I set off on tour) when they came to London to see a few modelling agencies with me, eventually signing with Elite before they moved on to a new one. Because I'd done it all before, I could help shape and oversee their careers, helping with contracts and advising them on what to take and what to say no to. Phoebe and Daisy credit me with teaching them the importance of working hard and earning money themselves, and I really cherish that. I never failed them; they tell me I lived up to that promise, which is so special to hear.

Fizz, two years below me aged 16, was now in boarding school and would come down to see Mum when she could. After all that's happened, I can see how Fizz's way of dealing with her grief looked different to how the rest of us were processing things.

Mum's death didn't seem to affect Fizz the way it did for us, but we accepted the guard she put up as her way of coping, even if we didn't understand her apparent lack of emotion. It's clear to me now that her way of handling the situation was to block it out completely. There were times when I consciously thought, *Fizz isn't expressing any emotion*, but like everyone else, I was wrapped up in my own way of dealing with the loss.

While working on this book, I came across an article online by Sue Ryder called '12 Things Young People Have Told Us About Grief', and I could relate to one of the points they made because I'd seen it in Fizz: the fact that everyone grieves differently and that's okay. We never made Fizz feel wrong about how she was grieving, but it would've been nice to come across an article like this way back then to understand that not everyone reacts in the same way. It would've been nice to also read that grief can affect a person's mental health, even beyond all the normal feelings of depression and anxiety. But I guess what's comforting is that if any of you are grieving or know someone who is, you've now got a resource in this book and through the work of Sue Ryder.

That article makes a few other useful points that I think is worth mentioning, like how young people often feel like the 'odd one out' with their friends when they're grieving, or how a person might feel 'boring' or 'too depressing' among their friends for speaking about their emotions or their loved one. There are so many little things that come up for a person when they're grieving, so many things that might make them self-conscious about their changing emotions or super-sensitive to things people say that weren't meant to be thoughtless or rude, such as, 'I understand how you feel.'

Another thing to consider is that not everyone will gravitate towards therapy, not everyone will want to sit in front of someone for an hour and talk about their emotions, which is why charities like Sue Ryder offer online communities and groups, and why there are other resources available online like scrolling through accounts on Instagram or listening to a podcast. I never want to feel like I'm peddling coping mechanisms or tools that are going to be a one-size-fits-all type of situation because the journey of grief is an individual process that is hard, no matter what. I only want to offer a load of suggestions that might feel good to you or someone you know. I really believe we all have the agency to follow our hearts and do what works for us.

Losing Mum meant different things to everyone, and for Fizz it was like she'd lost the only person who truly understood her. Fizz had her quirks from quite young, and she was always voicing the fact that she struggled to fit in at school, but she and Mum had an understanding, and when Fizz wasn't dealing with school well, Mum often moved her, never forcing her to do what she didn't want to do.

Fizz had always felt misunderstood, and Mum knew that. My sister often had the opportunity to take the lead on where she wanted to be schooled, so it was her idea to go to boarding school. Even though she was young, Fizz had done some research into a school that she liked and wanted to go to, and so Mum made it happen. I imagine making that decision was quite hard for Mum because she was quite an attached parent. She wouldn't have chosen for Fizz to leave her and board, but at the end of the day, she wanted to make her daughter happy and comfortable wherever she was.

Meanwhile, Louis was in the middle of launching his solo career when he found out about Mum's diagnosis. He had commitments with performances lined up, and Mum made Louis promise her that whatever happened, he'd honour them.

The strength Louis had to go through with Mum's wishes still amazes me because three days after she passed away, Louis debuted a new single he'd worked on with the American DJ and producer Steve Aoki on *The X Factor* called, 'Just Hold On', which ended up making the UK and US charts. That evening, we all went out to celebrate Louis, and to try and forget everything that had happened for at least one night. Naturally, the paparazzi had taken photos and there was some negative press and confusion from members of the public who believed us to be partying and having this wild time after our mum's death – when we were just trying to numb the pain.

After all that happened, we were so desperate to take our minds off everything, but from an outsider's perspective, some people saw those photos in the press and assumed we didn't care. Our every move after she died was looked at and picked up on. Of course, we knew that once the news was out, she'd be in the press, but it still didn't make having to deal with the situation publicly any less frustrating. It's hard, but I guess it's part of what it means to be in the public eye. We can't ever ask the press to treat our losses with privacy or even sensitivity.

I ended up being in Doncaster for a few more months after Mum passed. After being independent for some time, I can't say that I felt happy to be back home after everything had changed, but I knew that I needed to be there.

I'd lost the distraction of work but kept myself busy with the kids alongside Dan. There were times in the first two to three months where I'd not allow myself to get upset or cry, then I'd have these moments where it'd all come out, the most unbearable pain where I was having panic attacks and in a flood of tears. I'd feel better afterwards, until it all happened again. Each time it happened, I was inconsolable, and the physical pain of crying so hard felt like it would never end. I couldn't quite believe that I'd never be able to wake up in the morning, come downstairs, and see my mum, or never again have her at the end of the phone. When I think about her, those are the simple, normal moments that I miss the most.

I wish someone could've told me that it was all going to be okay, that I was going to survive this. I would've loved to know at that point that life after this was possible, because I was so sure that I'd never live a normal life again, that I'd never be happy. *I'll never get over this*, I thought. *I'll never be able to live without my mum.* To look at what I've managed to make out of life now, and to look at how happy I am, it would've been so good to hear that this was possible, but I had to go on to discover that.

Not having my usual outlet of work was having a negative effect on me. I could channel my pain into looking after the kids, but I couldn't ignore the fact that I was naturally work driven and ambitious. It was evident to my family that the past few months were getting me down, so decisions had to be made about what to do next.

Six months in, and the relationship we had with Mum's partner, Dan, was breaking down. We were all dealing separately with such strong and overwhelming emotions of grief, which had an impact on all our relationships. We'd lost the one person that literally kept everything together, and now life as we'd known it was coming apart.

We all had a different relationship to Mum – where us kids lost a parent, Dan lost his wife, Nan and Granddad lost another child, and it all equally brought a separate kind of weight that was sad and tragic to think about. Yet throughout such a difficult and stressful time, having Nan close by was our saving grace. I've never met anyone as strong as Nan, she's always been our superwoman, and the way she looked after us while coping with her own grief speaks volumes. I have no clue how she continues to have a good outlook on life even after losing two children.

Of course, there were times when Nan broke down. She'd lost her daughter, and now she was helping to take care of her kids. Recently, we were reflecting on it all, and it broke my heart to hear Nan say that she never used to understand how actors and actresses could cry to order; she used to believe it'd be quite difficult, but after all she's been through, Nan feels she could cry to order anytime. Nan says if she's busy, she's alright, but if she were to sit down and think about it all, she could get very, very sad. Even Granddad still finds it difficult and gets emotional, she says, and Nan wonders if it's an age thing, too.

I can relate to Nan when it comes to keeping busy – in many ways she and I are quite similar. Of course, it helped back in those days to keep the pain away and not dwell too much on what had happened, but now I'd say that keeping busy is more about redirecting my focus on projects or goals that bring me purpose, satisfaction, and joy. It's more useful for me to channel my energy into the work that I love.

Nan and I needed to think about what would be best for Phoebe and Daisy, as the little twins would stay with their dad. Before moving back to Doncaster, I'd wanted to buy a property in London, but when Mum died, I thought maybe I'd consider buying up north instead. Maybe the girls and I could live in that house together, or maybe it was best for Phoebe and Daisy to move in with our grandparents who could raise them. In the end, we mutually agreed it wouldn't be beneficial for me to give up my whole life to relocate to Doncaster. As someone who wanted to be a role model to the girls, showing them how to go after your dreams and build a successful career, it didn't seem right to put aside my ambitions at such a young age. Instead, we decided that Phoebe and Daisy would live with Nan and Granddad, Dan would look after the little twins, and I would pick up on the idea of moving back down to London.

As much as I've now come to a good place with managing my grief, Mum's passing will always be the saddest thing that's ever happened in my life. The way she died, how ill she was, and everything she had to leave behind, it's still hard to think about.

After a while, you push a lot of the memories down to cope with daily life. It's not just what I went through, it's what my sisters went through, and what Doris and Ernie missed out on, even if they talk about Mum being up in heaven. Now I can see that at this stage of my grief journey, just after losing Mum, it would've been nice to have had some support around how to deal with it all – suggestions of websites from bereavement charities, or access to therapy, or even hearing somewhere that talking about grief to family or friends can be beneficial. It would've been nice for someone at the hospital to have guided our family on next steps instead of leaving us to simply get on with things as normal. This is the type of work Sue Ryder has been campaigning for – clearer pathways of support for people to access.

It took losing Fizz three years later for me to seek therapy and talk about both my losses. Until then, I coped by bottling up my emotions, and looking after my siblings, which helped to push down difficult emotions that I wasn't quite ready to deal with. I focused on doing what I thought Mum would want me to do. It made me feel closer to her, made me feel like I was somehow filling her space a bit now that she was gone.

When I made the decision to leave Doncaster for my mental health, I was ready to throw myself into work and into creating a new London life. I thought attempting to look forward was how I was going to get through it all, but I'd learn the hard way that suppressing your emotions could backfire later down the line.

These days, Mum's death doesn't consume me on a daily basis, but I think about her every day. Just like Mum thought she was the luckiest before she died, I consider myself lucky too – lucky that I had 18 years with a mum I have nothing but positive memories of.

It took time to try and turn the negative things that have happened in my life into positives – I didn't get there overnight and it's something I've been on a journey to realise. But I can see how switching perspectives makes life more manageable and helps with my acceptance. I know it sounds clichéd, talking about turning the negatives into the positives (I sometimes annoy myself when I say it), but it's genuinely helped me survive.

CHAPTER FIVE

For the first year back in London, I rented a flat and asked Tommy to move down with me. He'd been a huge support through everything with Mum's illness and her passing.

Tommy worked in retail, so he was able to change his job quite easily and relocate to London. Lou knew how much I wanted to buy somewhere but advised me to rent first. That way, she said, I could get a feel for my area, figure out what I ultimately wanted, and save for a deposit. So that's what we did.

But I can see now that my obsession with wanting to buy a property was a distraction from the challenging circumstances at home after Mum's death. I couldn't forget about everything that had happened, but I could focus on having my own place and being where the work was. And there was something definite about owning a home – I was clearly looking for security and stability, after losing so much.

My year renting went by quickly. The flat I was sharing with Tommy was up for renewal, but I still wanted to buy, except by now it was clear that our relationship wasn't working. It was all just too much, and I realised we wanted different things.

Around this time, my best friend Brits was up in Leeds for university but wasn't happy. We used to speak on the phone all the time, so during one of our conversations, I said, 'Come down to London, let's find you a job. We can live together and have fun.' Brits wanted to do something creative like me, and I had loads of connections. Eventually, we set things up so that she interned at Lou's agency. When Brits decided to quit uni and move down, it seemed like the perfect opportunity to tell Tommy I didn't want to continue with the relationship.

Things with Tommy had come to a natural end, at least for me. I was so young when I met him, and we'd been together for three nice years, learning and laughing a lot together. His dad had also passed away, so on some level we could bond on that, but our experiences of grief were quite different. Anyway, it was nothing that he'd done, I think he just reminded me of home and all the tragic stuff that happened. I could see a disconnect forming between us, and I struggled to relate to him when it came to ambition. I wanted so much out of my life and career, while Tommy seemed quite happy to work in the same place for the rest of his life. Don't get me wrong, that's fine as it's what he wanted – we're all different and I don't see myself above anyone – but it was clear we weren't seeing eye to eye on long-term goals.

I had found myself in an unusual situation as a 19-year-old, working an abnormal job and making an abnormal amount of money. That was never a problem between us, but I was aware of how untraditional the dynamic was. Once I started finding my feet again after losing Mum, I knew it was time to break the news to Tommy. I felt so awful, but I needed to follow my heart and move on.

I ended up buying my first property in Hackney, a three-bedroom flat in the same area as Lou, and I was so over the moon. While Brits and I settled in, I focused on a new project. After years of posting content online and working with brands, I thought it was time to think about launching my own brand. I didn't know if my work online was going to be a forever thing, and I needed a long-term plan.

For obvious reasons, I'd always envisioned doing something with makeup, but the market seemed too difficult to tackle, so I decided to focus on tanning – another love of mine! Lou knew someone who'd potentially be interested in partnering with me. He already ran a tanning brand that was expert-led together with a premium tanning brand, and now he wanted one that was centred around someone in the public eye who already had a following. So, Lou pitched the idea of me working with him as someone who was savvy with Instagram and marketing, and could educate people on tanning through online tutorials, and he just loved it. We became business partners and Lou became the creative director for the brand.

My new business partner had the factories, he had the contacts and the retailers, and now he had the face for a new product. After a few conversations, we thought about doing a clear tan – everyone's doing it now but back then it didn't really exist, so in many ways we were creating quite an innovative product.

The biggest reason I wanted to create a clear tan was to avoid all the issues I used to have when I was younger. I remember going to the chemist when I was at school and buying the cheapest, darkest tan possible. There were times when I'd go to school looking full orange – the tan would be all over my uniform, my collar, and all over the sheets when I came home.

By this point, I'd probably used just about every tan on the market, researching all the products to find the best one for me. And I was tired of not being able to tan my face, and then trying to match my foundation to my tanned body. I was already a bit of a geek when it came to tanning so it was exciting to chat about it all and come up with ideas. I knew I wanted a more natural finish for our product, something that wasn't so obvious, and didn't leave traces or get all over the place. I wanted the formula to accentuate rather than completely change who you were or what you looked like.

Before creating the brand, I didn't realise that with fake tan, the orange colour you see during application isn't what gives you the colour; that's just a guide colour that companies put into the formula so people can see it on their skin. The clear tan we were creating would still contain the chemical that reacts with the DHA in our skin to give the colour, but we'd remove that horrible orange guide colour responsible for breaking skin out and staining clothes. I had very sensitive skin, so I wanted our products to be clean and chemical free, so it didn't break people out, and while we were at it, we could make the tan vegan and cruelty free, which was really important to us too.

In the end, it took us over a year to put all the ingredients together, but after lots of trial and error, we concocted the perfect formulas in our amazing factory in Glasgow, without compromising on our initial goals. When we were ready, we launched the brand in 2018, and called it Tanologist. Being involved in a new business endeavour gave me a reason to live. It gave me a purpose and a direction and tapped into my creativity in a new and exciting way.

Before the partnership, I hadn't thought too much about what went into creating a product. I thought you just made it and sold it. I hadn't realised how many aspects were involved like thinking about what goes into the formula, what the packaging should look like, how much it should cost, how to best market and ways to promote it.

Because my business partner already had the contacts and facilities, I could focus on what I did best: the creative vision. Apart from being the face of the products, I was able to test all the formulas, be involved in product development, brand building, marketing strategy, and events. I found the entire process so interesting, and it taught me everything I know today about creating and running a business.

Nevertheless, a lot of self-doubt crept in before the launch, and I kept thinking, *What if people don't want to buy it? What if people don't like it?* I still couldn't believe that I had the power to do something so big. The pressure of success really weighed on me because I knew that if it failed the responsibility would be on me.

My confidence took a bit of a hit after losing my mum because I no longer had that one person who supported and loved me unconditionally. I didn't have her around anymore to call up when I needed advice. She'd made me feel like I could do anything I put my mind to, and now I didn't have that anymore. So, after the launch, when I could see that the brand was taking off and that soon it would be a success, it gave me that confidence back. It became that one positive thing in my life that showed me something could finally go right.

Initially, we stocked Tanologist at Superdrug, and the brand went mental from there. Within a year, we were launching in different countries around the world so that we had Tanologist in big American department stores like Target, CVS and Walmart. And towards the end of 2019, we had the tan in Australia's Priceline.

Each launch had a schedule of events planned out where we visited the stores, and sometimes threw a party to celebrate. In Los Angeles, we had a big store event at Target, then had a big party in a villa in the Hollywood Hills. It was surreal returning to America and Australia to launch my brand off my own back, and a really proud moment too. I used to visit these countries a lot while touring with One Direction, but when we finished, I never thought I'd travel to these amazing places again, let alone stay in luxurious hotels.

I wanted to continue the lifestyle I'd been used to, but thought I'd have to come to terms with living more of a normal life once touring ended. Now I could carry on with that momentum of tour life I once had through Tanologist, and that made me so happy.

By 2020 we had 16 products in our portfolio, from the self-tan water, self-tan drops and self-tan mousse to a whole range of shades for beginners and pros. I loved it when people messaged me or tagged me on social media to say how much they enjoyed the products, how it made them glow, and how much clearer their skin was compared to other products they'd used. We liked receiving feedback from our followers and we made it a point to engage with them and establish a relationship.

It made sense that if we were promoting products to our fans, we needed to read their comments and implement some of their feedback. We heard our followers when they said that our price point was too high, and they couldn't afford it. A lot of our followers were young, so we brought the price point down so they could enjoy the product. If we didn't stay engaged with our followers, they wouldn't stay engaged with us, and if our followers weren't engaged, then what we were doing was pointless.

Running a new, successful business was amazing, and I liked having another project to work on other than posting content and working with brands. But being the face of a beauty product in the age of social media had its challenges and at one point created a lot of stress but taught me quite a bit as well.

Sometime in 2020, there were people online calling

me out for 'blackfishing', a term I hadn't heard of before. For those who don't know, blackfishing is when a white (or fair-skinned) celebrity or influencer appropriates elements of black popular culture for their own gain through beauty choices (like excessive tanning, wearing certain hairstyles, making certain makeup choices, and clothing trends and even filters). Blackfishing isn't particular to celebrities or influencers, but they're the most visible and obviously have the most reach.

Loads of high-profile names, mostly women, were being called out for either consciously or unconsciously trying to look more racially ambiguous after a thread on Twitter about blackfishing went viral, and then all of a sudden, people were accusing me and Lou of the same thing. People said we were taking it too far with the tan and crossing a line, which obviously shocked me as that had *never* been our intention with the tan at all. We were never out to appropriate a culture or disrespect anyone with our tanning choices, and once we picked up on the comments and articles against us, with people even calling to pull the tan off the shelves, we wanted to deal with the situation head on.

We felt it was our responsibility as a brand and as influencers to make sure we weren't offending anyone, and we wanted people to feel like they were being heard. We came out and did an apology – we pledged to be more mindful about how we tanned and represented ourselves moving forward. It was a huge lesson in recognising our blind spots too – as the name implies, sometimes they're hard to see – but it was a steep learning curve for me.

Looking back, I can see we had let ourselves go too far with wanting to be darker and darker even though we were promoting 'tan'. We wanted to show what our products could do and how you could get this transformation and achieve a bronzed look, but we weren't being conscious of how that might appear to other people who naturally had darker skin, especially as women with much lighter skin tones.

A big part of the problem was that we were self-tanning, then tanning in the sun, then using filters, so the content we were posting probably looked outrageous in comparison to our natural skin tones. We obviously looked a bit too unnatural, but it took our fans and followers to call us out for us to see that. Again, it was a bit like overdoing it with the filler. I didn't like feeling attacked by the comments online, especially with the tanning, and initially, I was adamant that we weren't too dark, but then after some time, I'd look back at photos and think, yeah, they were right.

As an influencer, it's easy to get swept up in beauty trends or social media bubbles without really being aware of how certain trends can get taken to the extreme or even potentially offend people. In some cases, it's like our followers bring us back to reality or open our eyes to something that's potentially an issue.

As a brand or an influencer, I do think it's good to learn from mistakes, to apologise when necessary, and to take accountability for our actions. I think it's just a sign of growth and respect especially when we're in the business of influencing. People won't always get it right and that's okay, but it's how you deal with it after that makes the difference.

*

Despite the opportunities coming my way – the kinds that expanded my horizons, teaching me new lessons and skills – there were days when I thought, *But what's the point if the one person I'd want to see this isn't here?*

Occasionally, I *still* think 'what's the point?', but since Lucky's been born, he's given me a new reason to keep doing what I'm doing. However, before Lucky, I had to keep telling myself that Mum would want me to take these jobs. She'd given me a push on this journey, so I had to see it through. And to make my life easier, I told myself that she was looking down on me, that she could see everything I was doing.

I used to have a lot of recurring dreams of Mum. They've become less regular now although they still happen from time to time. The most common one takes place in the house I grew up in (I always go back to that house in my dreams) and my Mum's still there. She's alive, even though even in my dream I know she's not, but she's in front of me, and I'm asking if she's still here because I'm shocked when I see her. I wake up from those dreams and in some ways, it makes me feel happy and warm because it's almost as if I've seen her, but at the same time, reality hits me and I feel so sad because I know that she's gone. Those dreams are so weird and hard to explain because in them I'm surprised that she's alive – it really *feels* like she is – yet I'm doubting it and wondering if it's real at the same time.

Loads of nice things were happening for me, but behind it all I was suppressing my emotions around Mum's death before going into states of complete despair. It wasn't a healthy way to live. As human beings, it's easier to push to the side unbearable emotions rather than deal with them straight on. Sometimes it can be too painful.

I was going months without crying, without thinking about what had happened, without even talking about it, and then something would trigger me and I'd sob for hours on end. My hysteria was a true representation of what was balled up inside of me for so long, and when it did finally come up, the pain and tears were impossible to stop.

Looking back, I wish I'd been able to feel those emotions along the way rather than pushing them to the side. Now I know that's where therapy would've been helpful, or at least talking about how I was feeling more to whoever would listen. I spent a lot of time in those days beating myself up in my head. If I was feeling sad and wanting to stay in bed, I'd beat myself up about it. If there was a day where I was feeling happy about something, I'd beat myself up and think, *You're not allowed to be happy.*

I didn't realise until after seeking help, a few years later, that it was normal to feel these emotions no matter how different they were, and that I needed to be kind to myself. In those moments, I needed to allow myself to feel a bit of happiness, and I needed to allow myself to feel angry or sad. It's hard enough dealing with the pain of grief without also giving yourself a hard time about how you're feeling from one moment to the next. My emotions were temporary, that's something crucial that I would learn. It wasn't permanent. It was normal to feel one way, one moment, and something else the next.

Whenever I wanted to connect with Mum, I'd pull out a special box she once bought me stuffed full of lovely things that reminded me of who she was.

It's something I still do today. She used to give me little things like handwritten notes that meant so much to me, and because I'm quite sentimental (a quality Mum instilled in me), I've always saved these things that were precious to me just like she did. Her notes would always make me feel good and bring a smile to my face, and they still do. It's all I have left of her now.

These days I keep the box at the top of my wardrobe. It's small and overflowing, and the lid doesn't close, and Lewis keeps saying he's going to buy me a bigger one – but I like how it is for now.

My special box existed *before* my Mum and Fizz passed away, but I know these kinds of boxes can be created even *after* someone has passed away. Sue Ryder calls them memory boxes, so for readers who might want to start their own, the charity has a simple article online on how to do that. With that being said, these boxes might not be for everyone as it might be too triggering. But for those interested, there are so many reasons why a memory box could be helpful, from giving you a sense of purpose when sorting out a loved one's belongings (making the process a little less painful), to providing a tool to help you connect with your loved one after they've gone.

Everyone's memory box will have a different purpose – some people might want to look at it often while others might wait a bit before they do so during their grief journey. It all kind of depends on how you're feeling and what emotions are coming up. If you do decide to put a memory box together, there are so many ways you can get creative with it – maybe you want to write your loved one a note or a letter just to add to the memories you've kept in the box, that's one way to try and process your feelings and connect. The way you want the box to look can also be creative if that's necessary for you. There aren't any rules to any of this, just ideas, and I know, for me, having something like a memory box has been so crucial to my journey.

Sue Ryder says a memory box can be any sort of 'container' not just a box – it could be a drawer somewhere in your house or it could even be an online blog. You could decorate the 'box' or keep it plain and simple, it's really up to you. And after you've decided what the box will be, you'll need to think about what to put inside, and this will be particular to each person. It could be something that was special to your loved one, or something that's meaningful to you. It could be anything like photos, cards, letters, a mug, jewellery or books.

You'll also want to think about a safe place to put the box, one that's easy to get to whenever you feel like looking through it. Regardless, if this is something you might want to do, it's important to go at your own pace with it all. As you can see, I'm *still* looking through my special box. Oftentimes it makes me smile and brings me close to Mum, and other times it might make me sad, but that's all a part of the process of losing someone.

I have another box full of cards because I can't throw them away and that started from seeing Mum do it, even though it's gotten worse since losing Mum and Fizz.

I hold on to things more now because one day those items might be the only thing I've got left of someone.

I've already started a box for Lucky, and it literally has his mouldy, manky bit of umbilical cord in. Lewis went mad at me for putting that in and thinks it's disgusting, which only made me laugh, but he knows it's important to me. I also added the pregnancy test that I wee'd on when I found out I was pregnant, and of course, there's lots of photos. I'm taking pictures of everything now, just like Mum used to do. All these things might sound strange but I'm thinking that one day, if we're gone, Lucky will have these things and it'll be special to him.

Whenever I look through my boxes, I fall into a hole of reading through some of the notes and cards people have given me over the years:

4th August 2016 – Lottie you have turned 18 ☺

Lottie,

From the moment I got you I was in love. From your big bug eyes to your little blonde bob to your long hair and gorgeous soul – you have been perfect.

Love Mummy & Dandy xx

LUCKY GIRL

To my Dot Dot,

You're the light of my life & my living angel.
Happy birthday. Thank you for all that you are
to me! I love you with my whole heart.

Love,

Your Phee Phee x

To Lottie,

Have an amazing birthday darling, sorry I can't
be there with you. We will defo celebrate when I
next see you and have a proper drink ☺

I'm so so proud of you Lottie. With how you
have dealt with everything. You're an amazing
person and so incredibly grown up already.

I feel forever lucky to have you ☺

Love you, oldest sis ☺
Louis xxxx

Dear Lottie,

Happy birthday! Hope you have an amazing day!

Thank you for being the best big sister, I couldn't do it without you.

Love from Fizzy xxxx

*

For a good while between the end of 2017 through to the start of 2019, my London life was all about working hard and partying harder. I loved going out and discovering London's nightlife because it was a complete release for me. I could put aside mothering and taking care of others. I could put aside the grief I was feeling deep inside.

Brits and I were out nearly every night of the week, which was obviously so exciting for us. I was 20 years old now, and finally behaving like peers my age. I'd never gone to university where most people get their partying days out of the way; instead I'd spent a good chunk of time taking on my family's loss and grief, trying to make it all as manageable for them as possible. I didn't want Mum's passing to ruin the big twins' lives, I wanted to make their experience of grief as gentle as I could.

I put a lot of responsibility on myself, but I know now

that I had no control over how others would grieve. Even so, I just wanted to make everything right. Now that I was living in London, and no longer in a relationship, I wanted to let loose for once but also escape as much as I could. It was so nice and comforting having Brits around to share my flat. I used to love us getting ready together for nights out, or the two of us bringing friends back to party. The nice thing about Brits was that we could travel back to Doncaster together, too, to visit our families.

I found it difficult trying to juggle my work life, my party life, and my family life. I'd be so conscious of wanting to go out on a Friday or Saturday night, then balance that out with heading up north the other night of that weekend so I could be there for family. I can't say I always got it right though, as I'd be hungover when I was there, and Nan and Granddad would pick up on it, with Granddad telling me off for always going out.

In my defence, it was a natural part of being young. I never considered my going out 'taking things too far', but there was a time when I started to realise the way Fizz was going out bordered on dangerous. I'm not exactly sure when my worry kicked in, but there were a couple of times when we'd go out together and I noticed her taking things further than everyone else. Even so, I'd sometimes brush it off, thinking I was just worrying too much. I didn't want to nag her or police her, and maybe I thought it was all a phase that she'd grow out of soon enough. At some point, it seemed like Fizz had gone from not showing or feeling any emotion around Mum's death to all of a sudden being hit by how overwhelming it all was. And in a similar way to not being able to understand her lack of tears at the beginning, now I couldn't understand her ways of numbing the pain. But Fizz was my baby sister, so I accepted her for who she was.

The two years between Mum and Fizz passing, I was doing so much with my career, enjoying my new home with my best friend, and finding single life fun.

On nights out, most of the event offers coming my way were either in Chelsea or central London, so Brits and I were hanging out more in those areas, especially Chelsea, and making a whole new group of going-out friends. We'd literally be out from Thursday to Sunday nights, making friends with the promoters, skipping the queues, attending events for free at bars and clubs, and just loving it.

We hardly ever paid for meals or drinks. We couldn't believe it. Our dirty raving days from when we were 18 were (almost) over and now we were embracing a bit of luxury and glam. Amongst the Chelsea crowd, everyone knew Brits and me as inseparable and there was no doubt that ours was a real friendship and that we always had each other's back. Like Brits says, if someone upset one of us, they upset both of us, and that's just how it was.

Brits and I travelled a lot together then and we always used to have such a good time. We've been dropped off in the middle of nowhere in Manchester in the middle of the night by an Uber driver after Brits gave him the wrong address – we were supposed to be going back to our hotel. Another time, in Ibiza, Brits and I were nearly kidnapped by a crazy taxi driver, which to be honest is funny now but at the time was really scary.

The two of us and another friend of ours had been at a club all night and were ready to leave and go back to our hotel. We were standing in this taxi queue when we jumped into any old taxi. Brits and I sat in the back, and our friend, who'd had a bit too much to drink, sat up front, just chatting away to the driver. Brits and I, who were a bit more with it, started noticing the driver making weird and inappropriate remarks, but our friend had no idea what was going on. Meanwhile, we were staying in San Antonio, at a hotel called Marco Polo, and the driver had come up to a roundabout sign that said something like 'left for San Antonio', but all of a sudden, the driver was turning right. That's when Brits and I were like, *Omg, what the hell?*

Thank God Brits was there (she's always been very good with this stuff), because she took out her phone and pretended to make a call. She was saying, 'Oh yeah, we're nearly back at the hotel. We're gonna send you our location, just wait for us outside.' Brits was proper egging it on, it was so great, and such quick thinking on her part. She probably ended up saving all three of our lives. The driver did a U-turn and started going the right way to San Antonio. He pulled up to our hotel, but as soon as he saw no one waiting for us, he sped up again, and by this point we were literally screaming, 'No, no, no, stop, stop, stop!' and Brits opened her door and started dragging her foot across the street. The driver came to a stop, I chucked money at him, and we all ran into the hotel shouting for security. The driver ran after us saying we didn't pay him properly, and we yelled back, 'You literally tried to kidnap us!' Then security chased after him, as he pretended not to speak any English. Brits and I were always getting ourselves into crazy situations like that but at least we had funny memories to look back on.

Up until that point, I'd never been single before as I'd been in two long-term relationships. I was trying to find myself, something that felt hard to do as I still hadn't found my confidence yet, which probably affected my dating life.

Let's just say that I got involved with a few wrong'uns at the time, boys who'd go on to teach me about what I deserved. After being in relationships where I felt I could be myself, I entered one that dulled me down and suppressed me as a person. Even though it was nice to be exploring, deep down I craved being with someone special as I loved being in relationships. Losing my mum amplified those feelings, so when I met my new boyfriend at the time – someone I was seeing at events and nights out – we fell into a relationship quite quickly. Too quickly. Naturally, I had my reservations about entering into a relationship with him, but I wanted to come to my own conclusions about who he was, and it felt right to explore the vibe both of us were feeling. Between pushing down my grief and becoming aware of Fizz struggling to cope, my instincts weren't as strong as they could be, and I brushed some questionable behaviour under the rug in exchange for intimacy and comfort.

My career had taken off as well as my personality and how I presented myself, but all of a sudden, I started questioning things I'd never bat an eyelid at before, such as what I was wearing. Anytime I showed skin, my new boyfriend would tell me it was 'slaggy' and embarrassing for him. Keep in mind I was pushing a tanning brand at the time, and there was no way I could promote it without showing skin.

Pictures of me in a bikini seemed to be a problem for him, and even a picture of me in pyjamas he didn't like because he saw that as sexual. Underwear jobs he really didn't like and tried to stop me from doing them. Slowly but surely, I was bowing down to his demands and making do with his controlling behaviour, which is shocking for me when I think about how I am now.

Brits, who was still living with me, helped me so much during that time, making me feel a little less crazy and confused. His behaviour soon caused issues in our dating life but by the time I was ready to address them and consider stepping away, Fizz tragically and suddenly passed away. Six months into our relationship, I didn't have the strength to mourn my sister and deal with a potentially messy breakup, but a year into us being together, I finally had the courage to end it, and my decision had a lot to do with being in therapy at the time.

Alongside talking about Mum and Fizz, I spoke about my boyfriend too, and my therapist could clearly see that I didn't want to be in that relationship anymore and that it wasn't particularly healthy. Being in therapy at that time, which I'll talk about more later, really helped me gain the strength and self-esteem to walk away and choose myself.

When I finally came out of that relationship, I experienced a new lease of life, and it showed me what I did and didn't want moving forward. I also realised that growing up in a big family, I liked being in relationships because I craved that one-on-one time, especially after everything I'd been through. I've always needed support from someone else, but being in a toxic relationship where my personality was suppressed made me appreciate being on my own for a little while. It also prepared me for my next big relationship.

Sometimes those difficult relationships are just as valuable as the positive ones because they show you so much about yourself. Looking back, I can see that at such a young age, I'd matured quickly between being on tour, becoming an influencer, earning a lot of money, owning a property, and losing my mum. So, it was natural for me to struggle to find that common ground with someone special, someone who matched my level of maturity, which is something I've found in Lewis.

It's so refreshing being with someone who's supportive of anything I want to do, and Lewis has no problems with me promoting underwear, for example, because he knows that if I want to do something no one's going to tell me no. If I'm comfortable with it, and the brand is well-established, I'm always going to take that opportunity. For me, a photo in a bikini isn't much different to a photo of me in underwear. I quite enjoy those gigs and work hard to have the body I have, so why not use it while I can?

Anyway, that whole chapter of my life is well behind me now, my going out days as well now that I have Lucky. I still enjoy a night out once in a blue moon – a nice dinner, a few drinks, just not the kind of nights

I used to go on in Chelsea. Honestly, I wouldn't even recognise myself back then, I was such a different person; not in a bad way, I was just young and exploring. It's all part of the journey...

CHAPTER SIX

Even though I was partying and having fun with Brits and my new friends, and navigating a toxic new relationship, I still couldn't shake this feeling of loneliness.

I didn't know anyone who'd experienced what I had, so I couldn't relate to most people on a deeper level. I felt like the odd one out sometimes, because most people I knew, who were my age, still had their mums, but didn't like bringing them up in conversation because I'd lost mine. Her death was like the elephant in the room.

My friends were as supportive as they could be, but no one had experienced the awful thing that had happened to me. In that time of grief, I felt quite isolated. Mother's Day used to be another day that drove home how alone I felt around my peers. Even those few weeks running up to the day were hard because of the constant ads in the shops or in the media, it all just reminded me of the fact that I didn't have my mum here to celebrate. In everyday life, it's easy to be hit with these little reminders that she's gone, but it's possible to distract myself now and live a pretty normal life. But in that run-up to Mother's Day, it's just a constant reminder that I don't have her here with me. It gets a little easier as the years go by, but the sting never completely goes away.

The sadness on Mother's Day still lingers, but overall, with Lucky here, the day has a whole new meaning which makes it easier to celebrate and feel happy about. I know some of my readers will have felt the same around Mother's Day – whether you've lost a mum you adored or had a challenging relationship with one. Mother's Day isn't easy for a lot of people for all kinds of reasons. It can be hard for mothers who've lost children too, and hard for people whose mothers are still alive. If you've struggled in the past or still do, Sue Ryder has some wonderful suggestions on how to handle grief around the day. I mention Sue Ryder because of my work as an ambassador with them, but of course there are other charities out there who have resources and advice.

The first piece of advice the charity gives is not to ignore or label 'bad' emotions you might be feeling on the day, like anger or resentment or sadness or jealousy. It's normal to feel these things, so try and be kind to yourself if they come up. It also helps to talk about how you're feeling, if you're ready and willing. That's a tip that's so important throughout the grief journey. Other suggestions the charity has is to write a letter to your loved one – that's always a good way to express your emotions – or join a support group, or speak to others who are in the same place you are. You could even ignore the day altogether, if that's what you want to do, and the charity says you could maybe unplug from social media and spend the day doing nice little self-care things. Just because the day might be important to others doesn't mean it still has to be important to you, or maybe it just means that you make the day into something that works for you.

In many ways, both Louis and I had the distraction of our careers and busy lives to help us put aside our loss as we managed our day to day. The big twins, Phoebe and Daisy, were being looked after by my grand-parents and were busy with school, and the little twins were with their dad and his new partner. Fizz, still in boarding school in London, didn't seem to be coping with Mum's death and needed help, something none of us could give her despite how hard we tried.

I kept receiving calls from her school saying that she'd not returned or that she missed curfew. I think that was the first time I realised how bad the situation was with Fizz, and as time went on, we noticed her distancing herself from the family or going missing for a few days and not responding to messages.

We could also see that Fizz was starting to hang around people who we didn't think were a good influence on her. People she met on a night out, or people who seemed to be older, and this worried us because they didn't seem like the sort of people she'd usually hang around with. We noticed her partying more and taking drugs, and it certainly didn't help that she was surrounded by kids at boarding school who had the money and the means to access all manner of harmful substances. She seemed to be doing anything she could to escape the pain of losing the only person who ever understood her. She started losing a lot of weight and for someone who'd enjoyed her food and was a healthy size, this troubled us.

Louis and I were doing everything we could to stage interventions, and as far as Nan and Granddad were concerned, Louis and I decided not to worry them too much because they had the big twins to look after.

They were also from an older generation, and we didn't think they'd have understood the nature of what Fizz was going through or how she was dealing with it. That's not to say that Louis and I could understand what Fizz was going through either – neither of us had the kind of mental health issues or dependence on drugs that our baby sister had. We weren't in her position, therefore we could never understand her reality or the dark place she'd entered in her own mind. This is why it's so important for people not to jump to conclusions about others, or to have so many big opinions on other people's realities and how they choose to live their lives. I think that about so many issues and hot topics today.

Louis and I really had to dig deep to try and see where she was coming from. We both went through stages of frustration, wondering why she couldn't get better, or why she couldn't just recover in rehab and be clean, but it doesn't work like that. We were frustrated because we loved Fizz so much and wanted to see her come through to the other side. We wanted her to be healthy and happy in her mind, but we had no control over the situation, and no idea what was going through her mind.

There were times when Fizz called me, having got herself into a bit of a state. I tried the best I could to console her, but it just got progressively worse. I wanted to try and understand what was going on for her, I wanted to do anything I could to help. I offered to have Fizz move in with me and Brits, but she didn't want that knowing she wouldn't have the freedom to escape in the ways she knew how. I found it hard that she didn't want my help, even if what I was offering wasn't going to solve her problems. At the end of the day,

I wasn't Mum, I couldn't give her what she needed, but it obviously didn't stop me from trying.

In an attempt to give Fizz some stability and drive, I tried to get her on board with my Instagram stuff. She came on a few work trips with me, and it was nice, but in the end, she just spiralled back into her pain. I used to encourage her to see a therapist, but the times we set her up with one, she didn't vibe with them, which made it hard for her to carry on. A lot of the time, I felt a sense of frustration at not being able to help her pull through. I wanted to solve her problems and help her recover, but I couldn't fix it, and I couldn't see why what I was offering her wasn't enough. I couldn't see, at the time, that her problems were much bigger than I could've sorted out. My solutions couldn't fill the void Fizz felt from Mum's passing, so she turned to stuff she shouldn't have to numb her grief.

Although we sent Fizz to rehab a couple of times, I personally never thought her issues had anything to do with addiction. I've always felt she turned to drugs because of her grief, because it offered her a temporary release. We sent her there thinking we could get her back onto a good path, and after those stints, she'd come out a more positive person, but it was only a matter of time before she reverted to the only way she knew how to cope. Her treatments would never be enough to help heal her.

My sister continued spiralling and by March 2019 we couldn't see how the situation would change. Fizz was no longer at boarding school, as she'd been politely asked to leave. In between rehab, Lou offered her a place to stay, hoping she could be a different influence on Fizz – maybe someone outside of the family would be less pressure for her. But no one could get a grip on her. No matter how much love, guidance and work we all offered to set Fizz on a more positive path, it would never be enough.

Lou remembers Fizz throwing house parties while she travelled for work (something I never had the guts to do) and I know she thought Fizz to be kind of a legend for generally pushing the boundaries – she didn't realise the depths of the issues Fizz was facing. She was always so respectful of Lou and was cute with her daughter, Lux, and in some ways, Fizz reminded Lou of herself as a teenager, someone who was lost, a bit goth, and into a more alternative scene.

The two of them would often have deep chats together and talk about documentary films on music. Lou would've had Fizz full-time just to keep tabs on her, but in the end Fizz ended up getting her own flat after her last stint in rehab, and that's when she started slipping from all of us. We couldn't really keep track of her after that, and as Brits puts it, she was here, there, and everywhere, always doing her own thing.

I had a trip to Bali coming up, which I'd booked ages before and spent a lot of money on. I remember umming and awing about whether to go because Fizz wasn't in a good place, and the last thing I thought was, *We could be in this position for years; I can't never go away or do anything ever again*, and so my boyfriend and I decided to go and have our holiday.

But three days into the trip, I heard that Fizz had gone missing and no one could find her. Friends were messaging me to say they were worried, and I'd spend the morning trying to figure out where she was. Her phone was off, and she wasn't replying to text messages, and I couldn't track down anyone she may have been with.

I was sitting on my hotel balcony when Louis called me to say Fizz had died of an accidental drug overdose. When he said it, I just remember screaming because it was the worst news I could've ever heard.

It was such a shock to think that my 18-year-old baby sister was dead. Over and over again, I kept screaming, *No, my baby sister, no,* because the thought that my best friend was suddenly gone hurt so much. The pain was all consuming. Even with everything that had gone on, I never thought we would lose her. I thought she'd come out of her bad place eventually, that we'd have only a few more years of watching Fizz cope with grief in the only way she knew how. I never expected things to end the way they did.

Losing Mum had been different because she was ill. I knew that death was a possibility even though I didn't really want to accept it at first. She had cancer, so in some ways I was subconsciously preparing to lose her because I knew what cancer could mean. But the news of Fizz passing away just like that was something else entirely, just a massive shock. She'd died just when we were discovering how special our relationship was. On some level, Fizz had been for me what the big twins were for each other and even though we'd spent a chunk of our time together in that 'annoying sister phase', through losing Mum and becoming more mature I'd come to realise the amazing bond we had. Two years apart, we had loved each other in our own ways, but now she was gone, I'd never be able to see our relationship deepen.

Just before I left for Bali, I'd asked Fizz if she was okay with me going away, and she'd reassured me that she was fine. She seemed to have been in an okay place when I left, that's why it was such a shock when I heard the news. Looking back, I know now there was nothing I could've done for her that day, whether I'd stayed in London or left for my holiday. Her accidental overdose could've happened at any time. All I wanted now was to come home as soon as I could and be with my family.

It was the middle of the night back in London when I

first phoned Brits to tell her the news. She'd been out with Lou and others when I called to scream down the phone that Fizz had died. Just like me she couldn't believe it. We knew she'd been going through stuff, but we never ever thought anything as bad as this would happen.

I called Lou after, and she'd just come home from her night out. She'd been aware that we were looking for Fizz that day because Fizz had meant to pop round to her house but never arrived. As soon as I called her, she said she knew instinctively that Fizzy had passed away because we usually only texted each other, never rang each other up, and if we did, we'd panic that someone was dead. After what happened with my mum, and the losses Lou had experienced, it just made sense.

When Lou answered my FaceTime, I just screamed in pain. She knew that I needed to get out of Bali and come home as soon as possible, but my boyfriend and I were in the jungle, in the middle of nowhere. It was like torture.

We ended up leaving Bali as soon as we could but sitting on the plane for 18 hours after hearing about my sister's death was horrific. I was in and out of tears the entire way, still in shock and feeling numb. I couldn't process what I'd been told. I didn't want it to be real.

Fizz passed away on the 13th March 2019, at just 18 years old, almost two years exactly after losing Mum. And as a family, we were back in that place again, dealing with another huge and incomprehensible loss. After those two difficult years, I was just starting to feel like I was coming out the other side of my grief with Mum. I knew I'd never really heal from something like that, but I was coping better and learning to accept what had happened to her. But Fizz's death took us right back to the start.

When I got back to England, Lou picked me up from the airport and took me straight to the train station so I could get to Nan's. I remember all of us just sitting around the table thinking, *How has this happened again? When is this all gonna end?* And even though we'd been dealing with a load of stuff with Fizz for months and months, the news still shocked us to the core.

The big twins remember Nan coming into their room to break the news. They thought Nan was coming to wake them up for school, that they'd overslept, but she was crying her eyes out, having just got off the phone with Louis. A day or two later, when we'd all come together at Nan's, Daisy said she felt as if she were sat at the table alone. She'd had a bad feeling about what might happen to Fizz for months, and I know she'd wanted to do what she could to prevent it, but of course there was nothing anyone could do. Daisy reflected to me that because we'd lost Mum, she just knew what lay ahead of her in terms of the grief, that it was going to be tough.

That day, as we sat around Nan's table, she couldn't focus or concentrate on anything anyone said. I could see that she wasn't coping, and we were all so worried about her. The big twins were just 15 years old at the time. It honestly felt like the world was against us. What hurt even more was the knowledge that the press were going to write stories about Fizz for the public to read and exploit, splashing her private life out there without considering this was someone's memory they were dealing with. My baby sister.

So many people were quick to judge Fizz without fully understanding the situation, or the pain she had been through. There wasn't space in those articles to unpack why she took the drugs in the first place, or to show she was crying out for help; there was just enough space to go into the drugs she took and how much had been in her system through the toxicology and autopsy reports.

The whole thing was quite invasive, and just added another sad level to our already awful grief. What helped though was the outpouring of love that came from fans, who have always been so invested in our family, and who were devastated by Fizz's loss. They showed us the same love and support as when Mum died, and their sympathy will always mean a lot.

The way Fizz's death impacted me presented itself in different ways. My 18-year-old sister's life had been cut short, and I didn't want to believe it. So on one level I was numb and wanting to get on with my responsibilities. I tried to suppress the intensity of my feelings through work, and so, just three weeks after she passed away, I committed to a work event that had been scheduled with a clothing brand called Revolve.

They were a good brand to be involved in and used to put on these big trips. Most of the time I couldn't believe I was working when I was contracted to do a job for them, so it felt like the best way to drown my sorrows. They'd fly us business class and give us a plus one, and take us out to places like Montenegro, Los Angeles and Bermuda. In Bermuda, they got us a boat over to a private island and we partied all day. The whole time we'd just be wearing their swimwear and clothes, with the photographer taking photos for their content. It really would just feel like one big holiday.

They also asked me to go to Coachella Festival in California. Me being me, I thought, *Yep, I'm gonna go. I'll be fine. It'll be a good distraction. I'm just going to a festival in sunny California to wear nice outfits and post content. What could be hard about that?* Three weeks after Fizz passed away, I honestly thought I'd be able to get my mind off the shock and the pain of it all and distract myself.

But one day during the trip, I couldn't bring myself to get ready because nothing felt right. I didn't feel right, and I hated the way I looked. I was crying, in a bad place, and working myself up into a state. Lou, who had come on the trip with me, walked into my room, and started crying herself, saying, 'You're not ready for this. You're not in a good place.' It took her saying that to make me realise that I'd jumped back in too quickly. It wasn't right, me being at the festival. Yet at the same time I hadn't wanted to miss such a big opportunity, and I didn't think I'd be any good sitting at home crying and being upset. I just wanted to try and forget about what happened, but I obviously couldn't.

I was desperate to snap back into normal life, and I think a lot of us are conditioned to think we've just got to get on with it. To a certain degree, getting back into a routine can help, but it's more important to listen to your emotions, and to let them show you what you need. The most dangerous thing to do is to suppress your emotions because that can eat you up inside and lead you to a dark place. It took Lou saying to me, 'You're grieving, you're in a bad place because you've lost your sister,' to make me realise that my tears weren't about how unhappy I was about my hair and makeup.

When I think back to that version of myself, I wish someone had told me about the five stages of grief: denial, anger, bargaining, depression and acceptance, because I was definitely hovering between the first two. Even though everyone's grief journey will be different, I feel like it's somewhat helpful to be aware of how your feelings could potentially fit into the cycle. I was grateful to have Lou around to recognise how I was feeling because I was too removed from my emotions to see them clearly or to even know what I needed at the time. I can see now that I desperately needed help, but I didn't know yet what to do or how to tackle the lack of control I was feeling.

Some months after Fizz died, I decided to take the big twins away on holiday for a mini break. I thought it would be a chance for us to try and do something positive and be there for each other. If I could take them away and cheer them up for a bit, then I would, as it was clear that we were all suffering and needed some relief.

We flew to Mallorca hoping a bit of sunshine would cheer us up, but when we got there it was freezing. Louis rang us to ask how the trip was going, and we told him it was grey and cold. Louis being Louis, he wanted us to have a really good time. He knew what we'd all been going through and felt we deserved a proper holiday, and within an hour, he'd booked us flights to Gran Canaria.

It was sad not having Louis there with us, especially because we knew how much he was suffering too, but we understood his work commitments and responsibilities for his little boy Freddie in LA. Fizz had turned to him a lot after Mum died but he hadn't been able to visit as much as he would've liked because he was touring, so losing Fizz probably affected him on another level. Just like with Mum, he had to carry on and deal with it while travelling, performing to thousands, and putting on a happy face. It would've been nice to have him there with us on holiday, but we were grateful for what he did for us and for the change of scene.

The weather was so much nicer in Gran Canaria, and the three of us had a chill time. We didn't speak too much about what had happened with Fizz, because I don't think we really knew how each other was feeling or whether we'd be open to chatting about it. We wanted to get away and leave it all at home for a few days, but we also didn't have the tools at the time to talk about our feelings with each other around what had happened with Mum and with Fizz. Eventually, I'd be able to rely on therapy to help me voice how I was feeling, but at this time, I still hadn't taken it up.

Now I can see that Phoebe, Daisy and I just weren't ready to accept what had happened. We couldn't accept that this was our new reality, that we no longer had Fizz. We knew what had happened – the funeral had confirmed it, solidified it – but we hadn't yet let it sink in. We were so heartbroken, and the worst thing was we still hadn't processed Mum's death; now we also had to take on Fizz's. It was just too much, too awful. Yet in that moment, we still had each other to lean on.

We didn't need to express the weight of our grief in

words. Sometimes you're just not ready to talk, and that's okay. The big twins were going through a hard time once again, and I just needed to be there for them. Being able to step in as that mothering figure – or just as their big sister – gave me a lot of comfort, especially since they'd now lost one who in many ways let them get away with cheeky little things I might not have.

Daisy especially was going through a bad time, and there were times when I'd sit next to her in bed through the night just to reassure her that nothing else was going to happen and that I was there. Out of us three sisters, it was Phoebe who spoke out the most if she was upset about something, and she'd often be frustrated with Daisy who she knew had loads on her mind but wouldn't share. I think Phoebe had the impulse to rely on people more than the both of us. As for me, I relied on the girls as a kind of crutch. I don't think they realise this but without them, I wouldn't have survived the way I had.

My anxiety went to a whole other level when I lost my sister. I think it must've been the nature of her death that caused it. I'd never experienced intense anxiety before, most of it was surface level, just general worry. But now, for example, if I were on the motorway, sitting in the passenger seat of a car, I'd suddenly convince myself that we were going to crash and that we were all going to die.

I couldn't even walk to a shop without thinking someone was going to grab and kill me. There were days when I wouldn't go out because I kept fixating on the worst-case scenario, and I couldn't control where my head went to the point where it became hard to manage. The anxiety started affecting my everyday life. What happened to Fizz was truly unexpected and shocking, and I kept wondering when the next big event was going to happen.

I didn't think I could tell anyone about my thoughts because I knew it wasn't normal, so I kept it all inside. My family were all dealing with the loss in their own ways, and I wanted to try and manage my feelings in my head, but of course, I knew deep down that I couldn't really do it on my own. Even though I had the comfort of a big family, I needed extra support to sort through my emotions. It also didn't help that I was in London, away from my family. Looking back, Daisy says it must've been lonely for me as Phoebe and Daisy were by each other's side every day and every night. I can't remember when it started, but I used to beg them to move down to London with me when they reached 18 so I could have family around.

Lou suggested I go to therapy. She'd raved about it before, but I never really took it on board. After Fizz died, she said, 'You know, it might make a difference.' But I wasn't that convinced. In my mind, I'd gotten through my mum's death without help, so I didn't need to go. I couldn't see how sitting down and speaking to someone for an hour was going to help me. My sister had died. My mum had died. How was therapy going to help?

There's been such a big movement around talking about mental health since becoming an adult, but when I was a child, there wasn't much emphasis on it. Especially up north, the mentality when it comes to dealing with feelings is often, 'Ah, you'll be alright', so I probably needed to hear from someone like Lou that therapy could work.

I had wondered what would've happened to Fizz if she'd found someone she trusted and liked. I also felt like I needed to be as mentally strong as possible for the rest of my family. I'd seen how quickly things could change, two losses in such a short space of time, and I needed to make sure nothing happened to me as well.

Lou had wanted her therapist to work with me, to see if I was alright, but that would've been a conflict of interest, so her therapist recommended another woman, someone named Charlotte (which is my full name), whom she thought would be good for me. Although I was lucky to have a recommendation from someone I trusted, I wasn't sure if the connection was going to be there – I know it's something that's hard to find, but something that's so important. I know now that finding a therapist for many people will always be a bit of trial and error, but it's definitely a good idea to get a feel for someone, and to work out if there's a connection, as you want to be with someone you feel comfortable sharing with.

As soon as I walked into my therapist's room, the weirdest thing was that she gave me a sense of my mum. I felt my mum's warmth, and my mum's vibe, and I liked how Charlotte was never pushy with me, just gentle. I was lucky enough to really get on with her, which makes all the difference when speaking to someone. It reminded me of being close to my mum again and being able to go and talk with her without having to bottle everything up.

At first, the hardest bit about therapy was just getting the courage to go to the sessions. I liked my therapist, but I never looked forward to the sessions because I knew I'd have to go to places I didn't want to go. She always used to say that if I wanted to come and just sit and cry, or not say a word, I could. I knew she wanted to give me the space to use the sessions as I wanted, but I also knew what it was like to block out my emotions until I came to those awful moments of feeling inconsolable.

Looking back, having that one session a week where I was asked about my feelings and encouraged to talk about them did so much for me. I used to feel much lighter after my sessions, and dealing with my pain head-on completely changed how I coped. Therapy changed how I experienced grief with Fizz. I think it shortened the anger period that happens with grief, and it helped me get to a place of acceptance faster.

It was just nice having someone there to speak to, someone who had an unbiased opinion about everything. I could dump what I needed to say, and clear my mind, and it helped make my day-to-day life that little bit easier too. It was useful lightening my mental load so that I could eventually make space for more light and understanding.

One of the things my therapist picked up on straight away was the fact that I'd not dealt with my mum's death. As much as I thought I had, all those emotions were still there, and they were getting pushed further and further inside of me. She inspired me to bring up my mum's death, to allow myself to feel those emotions, and to deal with them.

I could finally experience some closure around the long and scary journey I'd been on with grieving the loss of my mum, and I wouldn't have arrived at that place if I hadn't gone to therapy to discuss Fizz. Now, so many years later, I've come to a place of acceptance and peace around their deaths, and that feels good.

What's nice is that the big twins have also had therapy, which they actually started before me. Nan thought it was important to find someone they could speak to after Fizz passed away. I know for Daisy, it was helpful to have someone she could let everything out to, whether she was talking or crying, and that she appreciated being with someone who didn't know anything about her, who had no preconceptions. In the end, it helped her open up to other people as well.

It's tragic what happened to Fizz, and sad that she had to go through all that inner turmoil and pain alone. But as much as it's horrible for us not to have her anymore, I'm consoled by the thought that my mum at least has someone with her, wherever they are.

I think that's how we've kind of coped with it. Mum and Fizz were so close and so tight; it was almost as if they needed to be together. When Mum and Fizz passed away, they were cremated, so we've kept their ashes in a cupboard at Nan's. I've never been religious, and I struggle with the thought of there being a God when I've been through this much grief. Growing up, we weren't a religious family, but Mum gave us the choice to be whatever we wanted to be. She never had us christened, so we could decide for ourselves, which I think is a nice way to do it. But though I'm quite logical, I do consider myself spiritual in a way, especially since everything that's happened. I tell myself that they're watching because that's what I want to believe. That's a big part of how I get through it all.

Having said that, Lou recently reminded me of

something I hadn't thought about for years, something that speaks to feeling connected somehow and believing in something bigger that we don't always understand. Lou and I used to go to a woman who did our lashes, and one day, sometime after Mum passed away, this woman told Lou that her mum (who was a medium) had my mum 'come through to her'.

This medium wanted to give me a message from Mum, but Lou, who was a bit cynical at the time, shrugged it off. She thought the whole thing inappropriate and knew that I was still in a vulnerable place. But our lash woman wouldn't let it go. She messaged me about it, and the whole thing made me uncomfortable. Lou had to get in touch with her and tell her to stop, and to never message me about it again.

It would've been easy for someone with those gifts to target someone like me, whose family were in the public eye, who knew that my mum had died. Then again, I guess it was unusual that the woman who did our lashes had a mother who was a medium, who clearly felt the need to communicate a message to me.

Sometime after that episode, Lou and I went to have our lashes done, when the medium showed up to speak to me. I should've been angry, but I'd always been kind of interested in this stuff, even if I was sceptical. I'd done a few psychic readings when Mum was alive, and she'd always written it off as nonsense, so I never thought too much more about it. Lou told the medium to leave but she was persistent, and soon after, she sent me a message that stopped me in my tracks and made me want to speak with her.

She'd mentioned something about Mum that chimed with me, information that was relevant and true, so I went into one of the beauty rooms and sat on the phone with her for *ages*. She was saying stuff to me she couldn't possibly have known, and after we spoke, it made me feel better, as if the essence of Mum was still around. The medium told me that Mum would come through sometimes symbolically, in the form of a white feather, but I know spirits can communicate through other symbols as well. I think it's all quite personal to each person, if you believe in that sort of thing.

Then I started coming across white feathers here and there while thinking of Mum, which made me feel connected to her. When I bought my first flat in Hackney, Lou even put a white feather in there for me, which was so sweet of her.

The medium also mentioned flickering lights to me, another possible sign that Mum was communicating with me. It used to happen a lot when I thought of her, but these days not so much as I go about living my life. Yet recently, I was speaking to someone about Mum and connections with spirits when a bulb on my makeup light mirror suddenly blew out. I hadn't experienced a sign like that in years, so again, it shocked me, but made me smile. It reaffirmed for me that our loved ones are always around, and that it can be healing maintaining that relationship with them.

I'm sure some of this might sound unusual to some, but I do believe our connections to our loved ones don't go away, even if they're no longer physically here. I don't know how to explain it, and I don't have any answers. I just know what I've felt and experienced, and I know some of you will have had your own mystical and magical experiences that bring trust and comfort into your own lives. Whether it's religion or spirituality or whatever, we all need something that's much bigger than us to believe in.

CHAPTER SEVEN

A year after Fizz passed away, towards the end of March 2020, the pandemic had us going into lockdown. I'd come through my anxiety phase quite a lot by then with the help of therapy and had tools to avoid catastrophising the situation, but it was still a huge worry. If I did get Covid, I was realistic that I'd be able to get over it because I was young, but I worried for my grandparents who were older and more vulnerable to the virus.

Even though I hated them being so far away from me, I knew they couldn't go anywhere because of regulations, so I felt quite calm about it all and knew they were safe. Thankfully, I didn't experience any of my family being very ill, but I can imagine how tough it was for those who lost loved ones during that time.

Like a lot of people, one of the hardest things for me to wrap my head around was not being able to visit family. It was hard to adapt to how everything had changed, but once I got over the initial shock of the situation, I adjusted quickly. Therapy helped a lot, but what allowed me to cope even more was the new perspective I had on life after experiencing loss and grief. I knew how intense things could get in life, and how quickly and suddenly they could change, and in all honesty, going into lockdown and going through a pandemic didn't seem like much after the tragedy I'd gone through. I couldn't see how life could get any worse than what I'd experienced, but I know for many people, the pandemic would be painful.

Brits and I made the best of our living situation down in London. Because we were allowed one trip to the shop a day during lockdown, we used to go to our local Sainsbury's on the high street to buy all our favourite snacks. Once the weekend came around, especially over the summer, we'd go out, buy a few drinks, put some music on and sit outside in the garden making TikToks.

Luckily, work hadn't stopped as most of it had been online anyway, and brands were trying to figure out how they could still make money from people being at home. Most of my work then focused on sponsored posts, filming, and taking pictures for content. For Tanologist, I shot videos from home and played on the fact that while everyone was stuck indoors, they could make themselves feel good by putting some tan on and having a little pamper. And now that I was feeling a bit better about my grief around Fizz and Mum, I wondered how I could help people with their own experiences. I wanted to do something different with my time other than just working to promote tan or lipstick. Don't get me wrong, I love doing that, but the opportunity to do something more meaningful was on my mind.

I was carrying on with therapy online, and people were losing loved ones during the pandemic, and it just seemed right to use my platform to try and help others through a rough time. I could still see that version of me in a heap on the bathroom floor, who seemed adamant that she'd never be able to live without her mum, or cope properly and live a happy life. I wanted to show people that happiness, in time, could be possible again. I wanted to make something good of what had happened to me, to turn the negatives into positives, and give a bit of meaning to the losses.

I spoke to my agency about wanting to work with a charity, and someone mentioned Sue Ryder as being a really good bereavement and palliative care organisation. I especially wanted to work with them because of the services they offered with counselling. When I was looking into therapy myself, I was shocked to discover how expensive it could be and thought a lot of people wouldn't be able to afford it. I found out through my work with Sue Ryder that they offered free sessions, online workshops for counselling, and grief cafes where people could go and have a coffee and chat to people who were going through the same things. I wanted to promote the charity's services as something people could use that was more accessible.

I became one of Sue Ryder's ambassadors in the summer of 2020, debuting a mural in Aldgate East, East London, by the Graffiti Kings, artists the charity had commissioned for a special project. The mural was painted in blue and purple flowers, as two hands on opposite ends of the huge wall reached for each other, and the words 'Don't grieve alone' were graffitied in large white words. That work really spoke to me, so it was a real honour to be involved in the event.

My work with the charity came at a tragic and confusing time when there were hundreds of thousands of people losing loved ones and dealing with grief. The charity obviously had more and more people turning to them for help, and the least I could do was help encourage people to talk about their emotions and feelings instead of holding it all in and spiralling. It was key to my own healing, so I know how important it is for other people to hear.

The goal of the mural was to get people comfortable talking about grief, but to also give people the tools to help support those going through grief because a lot of people, naturally, don't know how to help. When I was grieving Mum and Fizz, I appreciated people giving me the space to talk about it, not necessarily forcing something out of me, but just saying, 'If you want to talk about it, I'm here. If not, that's fine.' I needed that bit of reassurance that people were thinking about me or giving me the space to chat about it or cry about it if I needed to.

Even though I've lived through losing members of my own family, it doesn't mean I'm immune to it or know exactly how to communicate my emotions. I still worry about what to say when someone else has lost someone. I don't want to upset them by bringing it up, but then I'll ask myself, *What did I want to hear all those years ago?* And it's always the simple questions like:

'How are you doing?'

'Can I do anything?'

'Do you want to talk about it?'

Basic questions like those really go a long way and let people know that you're checking up on them.

Sue Ryder had asked a few public figures to back their 'Grief Kind' campaign, created to provide tools for people to support family or friends dealing with bereavement. We were asked to come up with a slogan around something that helped during our grief and mine was, 'Just Bring it Up'.

Once some time had passed after my losses, I found it hard that people stopped talking about Mum and Fizz, people I loved, and it made them feel even more far away. Like I said earlier, this happened a lot when I was with friends who spoke about their mums. They wouldn't bring mine up because she wasn't around, but I still wanted to talk about her. I still have a mum; she's not physically here but that doesn't mean that I don't want to talk about my experiences with her or the memories we shared.

Other slogans to help people support those grieving were, 'Say Their Name', 'Do Not Avoid the Subject', and 'Let Them Know That They Can Cry'. I loved taking part in the charity's campaigns because they offered so many interesting and creative ways for ambassadors to talk about the people they loved, which gave me the space to keep Mum and Fizz's memory alive. The campaign was so simple yet effective, and it was also just refreshing to be open about my journey with grief, and to hopefully inspire others to do the same.

The act of 'bringing it up' is so important and can really give loved ones the time they need to release. Lou reminded me of a moment after Fizz passed away, one I seem to have completely blocked from my memory.

We were in the car coming back from a work trip, and it'd been a long day. We had about an hour's drive back to London. Lou was trying to see if I wanted to talk about Fizz, and she was asking me a couple of questions around the day I found out she died, and how I felt about everything. Lou had gone through a couple of losses herself, and as she said, if someone gave her an inch, she'd want to talk about it all and spill. But she knew talking about grief could make some people feel uncomfortable, so she didn't want to push me. But I must've been desperate to get my emotions out that evening, because as I was driving, I just started screaming. Back then that was the only way I knew how to communicate the pain, anger and sadness I was in. 'Why?' I kept screaming. 'Why?' I wanted to know why Fizz had been taken from us? Why Mum? Why me and my family? *Why?*

Lou's gentle questions led me to talking about every single little thing that happened. Lou had given me the space to express myself and to talk without trying to give me answers or tell me how to deal with what I was going through. She just let me talk. That's probably when she knew I'd benefit from seeing a therapist too, someone I could schedule in once a week to speak to about everything.

What I love about Sue Ryder is that they have accessible information online on what to do when someone close to you is grieving. Apart from bringing it up and letting people know that you're thinking of them during such a difficult time, the charity also suggests offering to do everyday, practical things for a person grieving, like cooking them a meal or tidying their home.

Another way to show up for someone is to spend time with them, if they're up for it, maybe asking them out for lunch or a coffee, or something else they like doing, such as a concert or a movie. Some people won't have the energy to make plans as they won't really know how they'll feel on the day, so Sue Ryder suggests letting them know what you're doing anyway and letting them decide whether they want to come. Whether or not people decide to hang or not, it's the invitation that counts, letting them know they're being thought of.

I think it's important to realise that no matter how much time passes, could be weeks or months or even years, whoever you're supporting will want to know you're thinking of them or that you're around to talk if they need and want to. People who are grieving will have natural ups and downs throughout the process, so someone you know might seem like they're doing okay, but deep down they might be sad or overwhelmed, which is why it's nice to have people reach out, even more so during anniversaries or holidays, which can be triggering.

Overall, I feel like it's good to try and read how the other person might be feeling, or to avoid applying pressure on people to hang out or talk or even bounce back quickly. Everyone's grief journey is going to be different depending on the relationship they had with the person they lost. There's no set time that a person will recover, even if time and tools like therapy can help.

I loved that the Sue Ryder campaigns were creative and interactive, and each one I participated in over the next several years helped me feel closer to Mum and Fizz in nice and simple ways. There was the 'Empty Chair' campaign in November 2022, when the charity set up a dining table and chairs in the Victoria Leeds shopping centre: 13 places were set for guests who had passed away, and in their place were images and items that represented them when alive. For Mum, I had her photo, a quote and a pair of midwife scrubs in her place.

The installation helped bring awareness to the little things we often forget or take for granted when going through grief. In this case, we were focusing on the impact of mealtimes and the loneliness or sadness that comes with not being able to sit with a loved one anymore. Sue Ryder's research showed that loads of people dealing with loss skipped meals because eating alone didn't make them feel good. Some people didn't think it was worth cooking just for themselves, and others found it hard to keep up with eating healthier meals. They also discovered that a little more than half of the people surveyed said it'd be nice to be invited round to dinner by friends or family for that extra bit of love and support. Something we did as a family during mealtimes once Mum passed away was to raise a glass to her, and this helped with addressing that empty chair at the table and how hard that was to see.

Where we can, my family still come together every year to celebrate Mum and Fizz's birthdays and especially death anniversaries. We all go to Nan's where she makes a nice spread, and we take the opportunity to rally together and celebrate their lives. Even though there are tears and sad conversations, there's a lot of love and looking back on good memories as well.

I recognise that not everyone will have a family like mine to celebrate death anniversaries as they can be triggering to begin with. Again, Sue Ryder has quite useful suggestions on how to spend the day, acknowledging that some people might want to carry on as usual with their routines so they don't have to think about it too much, whereas others might want to do something to remember the person and keep them alive. There isn't really a right or wrong way to do this, and it's more about following your instincts and listening to your emotions.

You might want to spend the day alone or take yourself out for dinner or a film, you might want to spend time with family or friends or start a ritual or continue with one. The charity mentions visiting a loved one's grave or the place where their ashes were scattered, if that's what you want to do, or writing in your journal to reflect on special memories and feelings, or looking through your memory box, if you have one. I like the idea of doing something they really enjoyed; the charity lists a few examples like cooking something they liked, or listening to a song they loved, or watching a film they always talked about, or reading one of their favourite books. If there was a place they liked going to, you could even visit it on the day. Whatever you decide to do, just be aware of the emotions that come up for you – anxiety, sadness, anger – and express it by talking to someone, working out, making art, doing something you love, whatever works for you.

It's often during birthdays or death anniversaries that me and the big twins will take to our WhatsApp group called 'Sisters' and lean on each other when we need some comfort. Whenever we're feeling overwhelming emotions, the first thing we'll do on those days is send a picture in. On important days like Phoebe and Daisy's 16th and 18th birthdays, the group chat was quite useful because it helped them deal, in some small way, with those days which were quite triggering. Because the big twins were so young when Mum passed away, they couldn't celebrate those days with her the way I was able to, so it was nice for us to be in touch first thing days before we got together to celebrate.

Another little thing we do on anniversaries is post

pictures of Mum and Fizz on our Instagram stories. I'm sure some of you will have seen these. I know it sounds weird, but it gives us a bit of comfort and contact with them. It helps us take the time to still acknowledge them, to celebrate them and express our love. I even used to post pictures if I was missing them, not only to keep them alive, but also as a release, getting those sad feelings off my chest instead of keeping them inside and pretending everything was okay.

No matter the day, it's always nice to receive that support from fans and followers, and I guess deep down, with all the likes and messages, all a person wants is to know that people are thinking about them during those difficult moments. It really makes a difference.

'A Sense of Grief' was a campaign I took part in along with other celebrity ambassadors and individuals the charity had worked with in the past. It was an exhibition set up at the Leeds Corn Exchange in October 2023, after the charity conducted research around how the five senses often brought up strong emotions and memories around someone who had passed, sometimes causing a sense of sadness or even a moment of connection.

The most common emotional triggers were, apparently, seeing an old photograph, hearing a favourite song, the smell of perfume or aftershave, seeing a recognisable place or touching an item of their clothing, and these triggers could be experienced every day or many times a week. As ambassadors, we were asked to choose five items that strongly reminded us of our loved one and that linked with each of the senses to put on display. For Mum I chose Versace Crystal Noir perfume for smell, wicker baskets (her obsession) for touch, Cadbury Dairy Milk chocolate for taste, the memory of her lovely soft voice when she'd greet me for sound, and all my beautiful brothers and sisters that she gave me for sight. It was nice being able to see all the different items people chose and the experiences they wrote about because it really gave you a sense of someone they loved, but it also brought us together in what is such a common experience. Visitors could walk around, view the items on display, read about them, smell and touch them, and it was such a nice way for people to be remembered, and for grief to be talked about in an approachable way.

The launch event for Sue Ryder's report 'A better route through grief' will be one I'll never forget. It took place in the Houses of Parliament in June 2022, and at the time I was 35 weeks pregnant (my baby bump was huge), and Lewis came with me.

Sue Ryder had published the report 'A better route through grief' around the campaign centred on the lack of bereavement support in the UK. They were looking to the government and healthcare stakeholders to create clear pathways for people experiencing bereavement.

When Mum was in hospital, we were surrounded by so many medical professionals, but no one ever offered us sit-down conversations about getting help. We weren't offered any literature, or information around counselling. It was clear that there needed to be better systems in place for people dealing with loss to know what options were available to them when going through dark times.

Sue Ryder put me in touch with then Shadow Cabinet Minister for Mental Health, Dr Rosena Allin-Khan, to talk about our experiences with grief, and to contribute to a call for action. It was crazy for someone like me, coming from an influencing background, to be working with a politician in the first place. I don't know why, but I had it in my head that politicians were a bit scary and a bit serious. But Dr Rosena was so nice and refreshingly relatable, and it was so good to work with her, and to connect with someone from a different world to mine.

Together we helped raise awareness around the issue and went on ITV's *Loose Women* to talk about it all. People are shocked when I say it, but I was so nervous to be on live telly. Despite the work I've done on my confidence, public speaking still freaks me out to this day. I found it hard to talk about grief, especially during a live broadcast. Not only did my nerves get in the way, but because the topic is so personal and emotional,

I had to try and keep cool and calm. What made it worthwhile though were the messages I received after from people telling me that they'd seen me and that sharing my story helped with their own situation. It's the best thing I could hear and makes me feel so thankful to be doing this work.

Every campaign I've done with Sue Ryder has given my losses a bit more meaning. They've helped me feel closer to Mum and Fizz and have allowed me to continue to keep their memory alive. I never thought I'd be collaborating with other people working to ease the struggles around grief, all of us connecting over such a universal experience.

When I contributed to Sue Ryder's *Grief Kind* podcast, I connected with a journalist named Clover Stroud, who I spoke to about my experiences. She understood my journey on quite a few levels because she'd gone through a similar situation to me, having lost her mum and sister. The conversations I've had with people I wouldn't have normally met, the campaigns I've taken part in, and even just using Instagram to raise awareness of Sue Ryder and their services has helped me find some kind of purpose for my pain. I know it's helped other people too. I get so many messages online telling me my work with the charity has helped them or allowed them to realise something they hadn't before.

Grief and death are such taboo subjects. No one wants

to talk about it or be 'negative', no one wants to upset anyone, or else we want to deal with it alone. But death and grief are such a huge part of everyone's life. We're all going to experience it, which is why I help encourage people to talk about it more. Ultimately, it's important and healthy to be open about your experiences, or to encourage others to do so, but of course there's no one-size-fits-all type of model.

During the pandemic, I wanted to help make grief less of a scary subject matter. I know it's uncomfortable, but that's one of the reasons it's nice to have charities like Sue Ryder around. If there's one discovery I've made, it's that we need ways of dealing with grief that are more engaging, creative and community centred. It helps to ease the pain and helps turn a difficult situation into more of a loving one.

CHAPTER EIGHT

During the pandemic, and at a time of my life when things were feeling more stable, I never thought I'd meet someone special or enter into a mature relationship.

Of course, I thought it'd be nice to start dating again, but it wasn't until I met Lewis and we started our journey that I realised all my other relationships had been a bit surface level in comparison. I had always craved that deep love with someone, where you're just obsessed with them and they're you're everything, but I'd never felt that before with anyone. With past relationships, I knew something was missing, and that they wouldn't be the right person to settle down and have a family with.

I could also see that although I'd been in quite healthy relationships with people, most of my partners had enjoyed drinking and partying. Looking back, I can see it was quite a big part of my relationships. Because of what happened with my dad, being around drinking has always made me quite anxious, which probably put a strain on a few of my relationships in the past. I'd always been quite scared about drinking because of the experiences in my childhood, but I hadn't really found a way to deal with my worry around it, so it spilled into my dynamics with boyfriends.

When Lewis and I first met at a club, we had a brief chat and that was it, but I immediately thought he was handsome and knew that I fancied him straight away.

I didn't really think those feelings were reciprocated though, so I tried to put it to the back of my mind. Some time passed, and we met again properly through mutual friends. Lewis and I instantly related to each other. We were going through similar situations as he'd recently experienced a tragic loss, and it felt natural to want to help him, and to share with him the tools I'd learned through Sue Ryder, therapy, and the two grief experiences I'd started to get to a better place with.

The way men deal with grief can look very different to the way women deal with it. The hardest thing for men is that they're expected to be the strong ones who hold it together or keep a family together, and that can be so much pressure during a time when they're probably not feeling capable enough to do that. It should be acknowledged that men feel the same grief as us women, as everyone, and it's about all people coming together to keep life ticking along as best as it can after a loss. When men are expected not to cry, that also impacts how they grieve, and to be honest, it's all so backwards. Why would our emotions be any different just because we're male and female?

Us coming together never began as a fairy tale. We focused on building a friendship first, and were there for each other through our shared experiences, but we also couldn't deny that we were attracted to each other.

On the surface, I saw Lewis as this big, tall, strong guy, but behind all that I saw someone who was quite soft and a little lost, and not where they wanted to be. I felt I could really see him as a person and what I saw was someone other people couldn't see because they couldn't look past his persona.

Something I learned through feeling safe with Lewis and establishing our relationship was how to tell when his grief was affecting him and what I could do to help him release. I understood that I couldn't be pushy about getting him to talk, and that I needed to give him the space and room to open up, if he wanted to. I'd gently encourage him to do so and let him know that it was safe, because men need that reassurance too. I know it sounds a bit old-fashioned but, truly, if you have a man in your life who's experiencing grief, it's good to remind them that they can be upset, and that it's okay not to be okay.

Because of the difficulty of Lewis' personal situation when we were first getting to know each other, the pressure would get to us. In fact, we had a few conversations around how much easier it would be to go our separate ways. Every time we agreed not to speak to each other anymore, that magnetism between us always brought us back together. We couldn't keep away from each other, and in the end, we thought, let's just be together and make a go of it. I'd learned by now that I needed to work hard for the things that I wanted, and one of those was Lewis.

So, by the summer of 2020 we had committed to starting our relationship, but those early stages were still hard because it was clear that some people in the public and the press were against our relationship from the beginning and didn't want us to be together. Despite this, my family were very supportive, which allowed me to continue trusting my gut.

I don't want or need to get into the particulars of the backlash from the press, as most people will know anyway, and I'm not here to upset or offend anyone. If I were to distance myself from the situation as an outsider, I can understand why some people in the public were put off, but I was on the inside, and I knew who Lewis was as a person and that we couldn't deny our feelings.

During those early days of our relationship, the pressure of outside forces really got to us, I'll admit, and we wondered if we should split up to make our lives easier. But we had an undeniable bond that we couldn't ignore, and ultimately, we had to fight through people's misconceptions of us. By this point in my life, after the experience of my last relationship, and the advice my therapist had for me, I felt more reassured about my decision to move forward with Lewis and must've known deep down, on some level, that this would be more substantial than any past relationship. My meaningful work with Sue Ryder and my weekly therapy sessions all helped to give me a more solid sense of who I was and what I wanted.

To the outside world, the nature of our relationship was seen as controversial, and the press continued to push false narratives of us as a toxic couple. I'm not someone who really gets followed by the paparazzi often. When I'm pictured, it'll most likely be at an event. But early in my relationship with Lewis, the paparazzi would follow us throughout the day when we were out, looking for drama and controversy where there was none, waiting for a shot of what looked like the two of us in a 'heated exchange' (as the press like to call it). One of the times they managed to do this, what they were really capturing was me literally telling Lewis that I wanted pizza for dinner, while he's telling me he wants a burger. We were having a natural disagreement about where we were going for dinner after having a lovely day, and the paparazzi were making it look like this huge row just to sell papers. It didn't help that Lewis is naturally very vocal with his hands, so when the press took their photos, people assumed he was being aggressive with me and speaking inappropriately.

The press were quite keen to push the toxic couple storyline which couldn't have been further from the truth. The way we were documented in those days was very frustrating, but there was nothing we could do about it. What we experienced with the press added a level of difficulty to those early days, which made me feel sad, especially considering everything we'd been through. Being followed by the paparazzi did affect the relationship in some ways because it made us quite anxious about going out. If we were having a disagreement, something every normal couple has, we'd then worry the paparazzi were going to catch it and make it into something else to feed their storyline.

Luckily, I don't worry about this now as we're deeper into our relationship and the press hasn't been so intrusive. By this point, it's clear that we're not in a show relationship, and I think people can see that.

After our engagement – which was the absolute best day ever – the press were after us a bit to get a photo of Lewis and I, and it was the same when Lucky was born for that first family photo, but I could understand that. In those moments, I don't mind the attention so much; it only bothers me when the paparazzi try to depict these false narratives of me and my family, or when my own efforts and achievements are overshadowed by my relationship with Lewis, or even Louis because of his involvement with One Direction. I've tried really hard to get where I am today and it can be frustrating, but I also understand the world we live in.

The work I did with Sue Ryder always used to get tainted by my relationships with Lewis or Louis in the press. I'd have to redirect annoying questions about them and literally say, 'That's not what we're doing here. We're trying to raise awareness for grief, and we're trying to help people, not discuss my boyfriend or my brother.'

I've always been very conscious of demonstrating that the name I've created for myself and the success I've found have all been down to my hard work, not because I was riding off anyone else's success or fame, which I think is the storyline the press likes to push out. As I've said earlier, everything I've done up to this point is a result of my mum pushing me to take my opportunities. She wanted all her children to create a life for themselves that was different to the one we had growing up without much money.

When Mum died, I had it in my head that I didn't

have anyone else to fall back on, that it was up to me to create the life I wanted, and in some ways, it was up to me to do that for my younger siblings as well. That belief in myself has been a life saver, even if it's meant putting a lot of pressure on myself. So, it annoys me when the press or other people try and take my own efforts away from me or try and make it seem like I haven't created a name for myself.

Sometimes I'll have an opportunity come in through my agency that I'll get excited about only to find out they want me to do a big focus on One Direction or Louis. And straight away I'll say no. If you don't want *me* then move on, I'm not the person for the job.

I'm very aware of where and how I started, and the fact that I had a leg up. I've always been so grateful for that. But when I'm working on an important project like the Sue Ryder stuff, I want to talk about the meaning and importance of it, not what it was like touring with One Direction or my relationship with Lewis.

A prime example is when the announcement for my book came out. The *Daily Mail's* headline was, 'Exclusive: Lottie Tomlinson documents 'highs' of touring with brother Louis at height of his One Direction fame and the grief she suffered following loss of her mother and sister in new memoir'. My first thought was, *Where have I discussed the 'highs' of One Direction tour life?*

I speak about the band in the context of it being the start of my career, how I met Lou and how I learnt about the industry and gained life skills, and how the experience shaped my formative years. But the press constantly has to spin that One Direction angle with me, and it drives me mad, especially because these headlines might look weird to Louis, if we haven't talked about it already, or to any of the other boys who see it, who might be thinking, *Why is she discussing details about the tour?* The papers want to spin it like I'm divulging tour gossip because it'll get them more readers and attract clickbait. Again, all of this just goes to show that headlines, pictures and news stories aren't always what they seem.

My relationship with Lewis never started off in a traditional way. The beginning was never light and fun and happy, and our circumstances had us skipping the honeymoon stage and going straight into some hard times.

We saw the bad bits of each other from the start. Straight away we were dealing with big, heavy issues like grief, which obviously isn't pretty, but I can take some comfort in this now – there was something quite nice about experiencing things the other way around because we had to accept all of each other from the beginning, even through our worst moments. It gave us a really solid foundation. From this place things could only get better for us now that all the difficult stuff was out of the way.

It made Lewis and I realise that we could deal with the big, scary things together, and we could deal with difficult emotions and feelings together, which only served to strengthen our bond. Some people start a glossy new relationship that's all sunshine and roses until something big happens and they realise they're not compatible or strong enough to help each other through it. It can be hard for couples who find themselves in that situation because they've been so happy when times were good, but then when times are bad, they find they're not equipped to deal with that side of things.

If we had a moment where things got on top of us, or one of us was acting up, we wouldn't let it affect our relationship; we could give each other a pass because we both knew we were going through difficult times and might just need a little space. Like I said, I've had to mature quickly because of what I've been through, and it was a relief to have this mirrored in Lewis and our relationship.

Lewis and I were quite similar in that we wanted that constant support, and we both needed a lot of love, and that's probably why we've stayed together and why we work. From early on we just spoke 24/7, figuring out that we were the type of people who needed a lot of care, a lot of gentleness, and a lot of love when going through tough times. But we also knew that we both wanted to be happy at the end of it all.

We both dreamt of having a family and a nice loving home, but when we first met each other, we never would've expected to be doing it together. Lewis comes from a big, lovely family just like me, and it was so nice to meet him during the pandemic in London when I had no family around, and to eventually become part of his own. Finally, I could feel a sense of belonging in the city.

All his family lived in southeast London, where he's from, so the more I went to visit, the more I loved the area they lived in, which is more suburban and much quieter. Not too long into our relationship, I made quite an impulsive move and decided to buy a property in the area. I didn't have anything tying me down to Hackney, and I kind of just thought, *What's the worst that can happen? If all else fails, it'll just be my investment.* Initially, I was looking for something that was done up and ready, something I could be happy with, but I couldn't find anything that fitted my style. Then one day, Lou said to me, 'Why don't you just buy a doer-upper?'

'Do you think I'd actually be able to do it?' I asked. I'd obviously never done something like this before or even thought about doing it, so I didn't know where I would start.

'You'll do it,' she said. 'You'll be fine, I'll help you.'

I went looking for something I could renovate and found this 1960s style house with a flat roof, and straight away I saw this vision for it. It wasn't the type of house you'd see often in the UK, and I thought to myself, I bet I could make this look like a villa in Ibiza or LA.

By this time, I'd left Hackney to move in with Lewis and be closer to his family. We decided to take on the project of doing up the house together, but it was a lot more work than we thought it would be. Regardless, it turned out to be one of the best projects I've ever worked on and came with such a sense of achievement. I worked alongside an architect to design everything as I wanted it, and they really helped me bring my vision to life.

Lewis and I had envisioned getting the house and enjoying it together for a while before trying for a baby. We always spoke about having a big family of our own but had a specific timeline in mind to start at the end of 2022. Lewis and I had bonded over family even as friends. He knew how big my family was and how much they meant to me. He knew everything I'd been through and how much I adored babies. And I knew how close he was to his own family, and how much he admired his brother, who had a lovely wife and three children of his own.

We spoke about our values and what we wanted from life from the start, but never suspected we'd achieve those things together, even though we were so obviously aligned about settling down one day with someone special and having children. We must've thought, deep down, we could do it together, but it seemed like early days back then to be jumping to conclusions about how our relationship would develop. Now that we were progressing and our feelings for each other were quite clear, we wanted to create the kind of life we both craved, making the most of what we found in each other.

We wanted the timing to be right, but as soon as I began overseeing the renovations to the house, I realised I was pregnant with Lucky and that our plans were happening a year earlier than expected. I'd now be having a baby in the summer of 2022! The day I found out – three weeks before Christmas – I remember running to Lewis with my pregnancy test and crying, completely shocked and scared.

'What's wrong, what's wrong?' he asked.

'Omg,' I cried, panicking about how we hadn't planned this, and how we'd just been enjoying our time together and having all these nights out. The pregnancy was so unexpected, and I didn't know if the timing was right, but now I realise there's never a right time. I thought Lewis would be having the same thoughts as me, but he was genuinely excited when I told him. He had no doubts in his head.

Of course I'd always been maternal, having wanted

a baby for as long as I could remember. Phoebe and Daisy used to beg me for ages to have one because they wanted a little niece or nephew, and it felt like the whole family were counting on me to do it. The idea of being a mum and creating that family unit excited me, and I was now with someone I could see myself settling down with, but was I ready?

Over the next few days, my fears came to the front of my mind. I was still only 23 years old, focusing on my career and in this new relationship. I was still going out partying, and now all of a sudden I wouldn't be able to go out at all, or even go on my photoshoots. I'd also be putting on weight, which I knew could be triggering given the issues I'd had when I was younger. But after every day that went by, we saw ourselves re-evaluating our whole life and re-planning it all. And as soon as I went up north for the Christmas holidays, I told the big twins the news because I knew how excited they would be (although I didn't tell the rest of the family just yet). Phoebe and Daisy were absolutely buzzing. It was the best feeling. I was finally making their dreams come true, as well as mine.

CHAPTER NINE

Lewis and I were having a baby, and it was time to get our heads around that. I wondered how I would adapt my life for this person who was the size of a grain of sand. I'm not one of those who's naturally slim, so I've had to work quite hard to make sure I stayed that way, and so being pregnant came with a new set of challenges.

I loved carrying Lucky up until the end (when my body, physically and emotionally, couldn't take it anymore), but I had to come to terms with my relationship to food and my body overall. Before starting my wellness business, Verdure, and learning about nutrition and maintaining a healthy lifestyle, I used to binge eat quite a lot, which probably backfired on me during my pregnancy. If I had a shoot, an event or a trip booked,

I'd go mental for about two weeks restricting my diet, and then afterwards I'd be so desperate for food I'd have a big binge, only to go back to square one.

As soon as I found out I was pregnant, I thought, *There's no reason to watch what I eat now*. I got excited about that because one of my pleasures in life is food. I know some people aren't fussed either way and just eat to survive, but I love food, and it's the same for Lewis. Right from the start, I used the pregnancy as an opportunity to indulge.

My cravings came on straight away, and I couldn't help myself with what I wanted to eat, and I couldn't restrict my food the way I used to. I craved a lot of cereal, not the healthy, nutritional stuff, but the chocolatey, sugary ones. I'd wake up in the morning and eat so much of it. I craved carbs like bagels and toast. Cakes and cookies. I ate footlongs from Subway and full pizzas from Domino's. I became obsessed with chocolate. I wanted it all the time.

Chocolate is something I never used to crave before the pregnancy, but I've carried on with it now, which is weird because I'd always been more of a sweets person, like gummies or sours, but that didn't appeal to me during the pregnancy. I literally just ate anything that was processed and unhealthy. On top of that, the bigger my bump grew, the less motivation and energy I had to keep up with going to the gym. I also wasn't educated enough to know what exercises I could do and didn't want to do anything that might affect my baby. So, at some point, I stopped exercising.

My work changed because I couldn't go out and shoot certain things, and reality as I knew it came to a stop. I'd gone from going out and living the high life to not being able to do much of anything, so junk food was my happiness. I'd wait for Lewis to leave for work and then I'd sit there and scoff my face. He used to come home, and I'd be troughing on a full Domino's. He couldn't believe his eyes with some of the things I was eating or how I was eating because it was so different to how I usually ate. I couldn't help myself, but in the end, it affected him too and he ended up gaining weight, about 20kg.

It's not like Lewis and I didn't ever eat these things, but it would be the occasional treat, otherwise we focused on being as healthy as possible. When Lucky was on the way we lost the plot a bit and overindulged. We honestly laugh so much now thinking about how we used to scoff our faces.

Of course there were many positive things about being pregnant. After all, it had always been my dream.

It made me feel close to Mum, for one thing, especially when I found out I was having a little boy. It came as a shock to me because I'd convinced myself I was having a little girl, something I always wanted. (Now, I can't even imagine having a little girl, but I definitely want one in the future.)

As a young girl myself, I aspired to be like my mum, who I still consider a role model, so when I knew I was having Lucky, it felt as if I were stepping into Mum's shoes as her first child was a little boy too. Having a son showed me that you don't always know what you need.

The nine months of carrying Lucky and becoming a parent after was bittersweet because even though I felt that closeness with Mum, I was sad that she couldn't be with me on the journey. I wanted her to *see* me. She knew how much I wanted to be a mum, and I often thought about how happy she would've been to see me pregnant. And as a midwife, she would've been the perfect person to help me through everything.

I had all these questions for her that I knew she'd have the answers to, but I couldn't ask them because she wasn't here, and that was incredibly hard. During the pregnancy, I wanted to ask if this was normal or that was normal. I knew how much experience she had with pregnancy and childbirth because of her work – and the fact that she'd given birth to seven children! I worried a lot throughout the pregnancy, but the low-level anxiety was standard. I wondered if Lucky was okay and if he was getting everything he needed nutritionally, and then once he started moving around, the sensation felt amazing, but I grew paranoid. If his movements were fewer than another day or weren't happening at a certain time, I wondered if everything was okay.

It was an emotional time, and it was sad not to have Mum with me, but Lewis was incredible as were the rest of my family. They carried me through the difficult times and made me focus on the positives of getting to be a mum, something I'd wanted for so long.

I expected to swell up but, despite my appetite, I didn't expect to double in weight, gaining almost four stone by the end of my pregnancy. I never had any sickness through my first trimester, so all the food I was eating was going in, and the weight was adding up – it didn't help that I was eating rubbish and not working out.

Trying to accept the weight gain came in stages. Early on, I noticed quite quickly that I was gaining weight, and I struggled with that, realising I didn't have the inner confidence I probably thought I did. I was still so tied up in my physical appearance, which I thought was everything. I honestly thought, *If I don't look good, I'm not going to be happy, I'm not going to have any work, and people won't want to work with me.* I had those thoughts in my head a good majority of my pregnancy, which didn't help.

I'd put on a bit of weight, go into shock about it, then get used to it for a while. When the bump came, I embraced it, and there was a period in the middle of my pregnancy where I'd come to terms with putting on the weight and enjoyed being able to grow my own baby. But then towards the end, the weight had become quite a lot, and my bump was huge. My face had blown up and all the rest of it. Physically, I was so uncomfortable, my hands and feet had swollen up like balloons. I could hardly walk properly, and just about waddled everywhere. Lewis was so lovely to me throughout it all, even when I was huge. He'd tell me I was so beautiful and make me feel so good about myself. Even when I felt my lowest with all the physical and emotional changes, he was picking me up and making me feel special. When my feet were humungous, he used to get them up on a pillow and massage them for me. He was so cute and helped me kind of accept the situation for what it was and focus on the end goal.

The last few weeks of my pregnancy, I was so upset with my body, I just wanted Lucky out so I could get rid of the weight, and all the physical discomfort, which kind of ruined the end of the pregnancy for me. I regret how I was about it now as I know I couldn't prevent what happened, but I know I could have made better decisions around what I was eating.

The massive weight gain in combination with all the fillers I'd had before getting pregnant made me feel really insecure. The fillers in my lips and cheeks made me look silly as my face blew up, and it was then that I realised the beauty treatments had got a bit out of control.

After having Lucky, I got rid of them all. It happened to coincide with a movement online supporting a more natural look, which helped me take the plunge. I think it was carrying Lucky and having to reckon with my body that started this journey of self-acceptance. I thought of Lucky one day having to go through these same feelings I was going through, and it made me upset. It got me questioning why I had these feelings in the first place – I knew so much of it was because of my career and social media. I could see beyond that now for the first time, that there was something so much more important because my body had created life.

Even though I had a hard time with my body developing, now I also had an appreciation for it. My body was growing a healthy baby, and later, when I began breastfeeding him, I thought, my body is literally *giving* my child life, and all these realisations kicked off this path in me around this inner self-acceptance and confidence that up until that point I still hadn't gained.

Luckily, I was able to give birth naturally, something I'd always wanted to experience. The idea of having a C-section and going through major surgery didn't appeal to me. If I had a C-section, I wouldn't be able to pick my baby up for a few weeks or drive or be able to go to the gym as quickly as I wanted, so I was *adamant* about not having one.

But at around 37 weeks pregnant, I couldn't feel

Lucky moving as much, and so the doctors decided to induce me because it was the safest thing to do. By this point, if Lucky wasn't ready to come out, it would be harder to get the labour going naturally, but like I said, I was determined to avoid having a C-section at all costs.

I'd been told that one thing I could do to make sure the baby came down was to keep active, so I *literally* didn't stop moving. The nurses at the Portland Hospital had never seen anything like it. They would come in and see me hopping on a bouncy ball, walking laps in my room, I even walked right down to Oxford Street and back. Lewis couldn't believe it – especially as I'd barely done anything in the last few months. As I hobbled along with my bump thinking, *This baby will come out, this baby will come out!* strangers were asking me if I was alright. But after two days of activity and determination, nothing happened. I was contracting but not dilating, and I needed to be at least 2cm to break my waters.

One evening, the staff told me to go to sleep and that in the morning I might have to have a C-section because they couldn't carry on with the induction if I wasn't dilating. I grew upset. I remember deciding to go for one last walk, and on that walk, I remember thinking, however silly it sounds, *Why hasn't Mum helped me with this? She'd know how much I'd want to give birth naturally.* And then as I kept walking, I said, 'Can you just *please*, like, help me?' I came back to my room, tired, and went to bed, and an hour later, my waters broke.

They gave me strong pain relief and an epidural, and even though I was only in active labour for five hours, there was a moment when they started dressing me for a C-section because Lucky's heart rate was dropping. They needed to get him out, and when the consultant came to check on me one last time, knowing I didn't want that C-section, he said, 'You're 10cm, so let's get your legs up and push.'

As soon as Lewis heard those words, he started going all funny. 'I don't think I'm ready...' he said.

'Babe, we're ready! You can't wait on this!'

As soon as I heard my baby's heart rate was dropping, I pushed for my life but because I was numb from the waist down from the epidural, I couldn't feel anything. I was pushing with everything I had, and the midwives were telling me to have a break, but all I could think was, *I've got to get this baby out.*

During my growth scans, where the nurses monitor the baby's growth and predict how much he or she might weigh, I was told during my third trimester that my baby was going to be huge and that I'd struggle to push him out because of his abnormally big head. Imagine telling that to a pregnant woman that's got to then push that baby out! They were telling me he was going to be 8lb plus, so I was terrified of having to deliver him!

Then Lucky was born. 6am *on the dot* (this always makes me laugh) at 6lb 8oz. My little boy, so tiny! I didn't think he was mine – this whole time I'd envisioned them passing me a massive baby, but since then, I've read and heard from other women that it's normal for those growth scans to be inaccurate. I haven't been the only mum slightly confused by the baby in her arms.

It had taken me about 10 minutes of pushing, but when he finally came, he wasn't breathing at first and it was awful. They started pulling the buzzer, and everyone started running in. Lucky was all limp, and I was having a panic attack because they wouldn't bring him to me. They had put him on me for like a minute before taking him away again, but soon after Lucky came around. My baby had just been shocked by how quickly he'd come out. Even though I found that part of the experience a bit traumatic, I loved the actual process of giving birth, and it was so amazing to have first-hand experience of something I'd been fascinated by since I was a kid.

We decided on the name Lucky halfway through the pregnancy. There were a few names picked out already, but when I heard that Lewis was working on a business deal with a man whose business partner was named Lucky, I just thought, *I love that name so much*, and thought it was so cute (the man was Indian, and his full name was Lakhbir, but he shortened it to Lucky).

Of course, I had a few doubts about it just because I knew it would be an unusual name for a lot of people, but I thought, *Why not add the name to our list anyway?* We had three possible names, so we decided to wait until he was born to see. Just after I gave birth, Lewis was filming, and he said, 'Right, what's he called? Whatever you say on this video is gonna be his name.' And I said, 'He's Lucky,' and that was it.

Our son's always been little Lucky, and now it makes sense because of everything that's happened in my life. And the funny thing is, some weeks after giving birth, I posted a picture on Instagram, and one of my followers asked if I'd named him Lucky because of Fizz. I had no idea that the Latin roots of Félicité's name (Felicitas) meant lucky, so it floored me for a second. But it was such a lovely coincidence and made me feel closer to both Mum and Fizz.

After giving birth, I thought I'd be in a baby bubble, those first special weeks where after waiting for so long you finally get to be with your baby. Instead, there were so many intense emotions that came just after giving birth, and I was met with the baby blues, which surprised me.

It made sense that because I'd spent five hours in active labour on all these drugs my body was completely overwhelmed. Now that I had my baby and was slowly coming off the medication, my body, my brain and my nervous system needed time to adjust. I remember being such a nervous wreck those few days after.

On our way back home from the hospital, I made Lewis drive 20mph the whole way. Even though Lucky was in his car seat, I was crying out with each little speed bump. The adrenaline I'd had during the birth wasn't wearing off, and I couldn't help but feel scared something was going to happen to my baby. I never could've prepared for that feeling of all of a sudden having him in the world after being protected inside me for so long. I think a lot of suppressed feelings came out at that time too, but I couldn't help it. Lucky was so tiny and delicate, all 6lb 8oz of him.

The first five days I spent crying the whole time. I was so tired and so exhausted, but I couldn't sleep because of the adrenaline. I didn't dare go to sleep when Lucky slept because I thought something might happen to him in the night, and I refused to turn the lights off so I could always see him. But after my hormones levelled out, that rollercoaster of emotions subsided.

I can't even imagine how hard it must be for women who experience post-natal depression, something that can happen after that period of the baby blues, which typically only lasts for a week or two. There was something so upsetting about knowing how excited I'd been to have my baby, only for him to come and for me to experience the complete opposite for those first few weeks.

I think it's common for women to think that they're automatically going to be in this brilliant and lovely baby bubble once they give birth, and that it's all going to be amazing, but it's not always like that at first. Throughout it all, Lewis was so supportive, so calm and level-headed about stuff while I just panicked. The tables had reversed. During my pregnancy, Lewis talked about how he wasn't going to cope when Lucky arrived, how he'd worry so much, and at the time, I was quite chilled about it all, saying, 'It's fine, you just have to trust that the baby will be okay and that you're equipped to look after him.' Back then, I was reassuring Lewis, and now he was reassuring me.

I couldn't even look at Lucky without crying because I loved him that much. I remember thinking, *I'm literally putting my whole life in your hands because if anything ever happens to you, I'll never survive losing you*, and that was such a scary thought. It's hard to comprehend the idea of anything ever happening to a child, especially after experiencing the worst things that could ever happen, twice. I knew how real it could all be. And it really hit home just what my nan and granddad went through all those years ago when they lost their son, Jonathan. But Lewis reminded me that most people survive these feelings, that they pull through and that Lucky would be okay. Eventually I started settling in, finding my feet, and getting my energy back.

Learning to be with Lucky came naturally but it had its minor challenges. I found myself struggling with breast feeding and not knowing what to do but having to figure it out myself.

I went into the experience of having him quite blind because I didn't do much research. Being one of seven and having watched my mum bring up the smaller kids and knowing I was good with babies, I just thought I'd be fine and that I'd instinctively know what I was doing, which I regret a little now. It was pretty naïve.

Psychologically, I think not having my mum around put me in a place where I didn't want to ask anyone else for help. I grew stubborn about it and thought, *If I can't ask her, I'm going to deal with it myself,* which obviously hindered me in a lot of ways. Yet at the same time, I know I could've done hours and hours of research but until Lucky arrived and I was looking after him, I was never going to learn fully.

For me, the hardest part of becoming a mum really has been not having my own around to witness it. She would've loved Lucky so much, and I know that he's missing out on having her because she was so special to me. But I'm already talking to him about his nanny up in heaven.

Obviously, he doesn't understand yet but whenever we pass by pictures of her in the house, I speak of Mum and want to make sure that he always knows about her. There's no reason why she can't be a part of his life still just because she isn't physically here. I want him to know how much she meant to me and how much he would've meant to her.

The thought of Mum adoring him can be really overwhelming, especially when I think about how much I love him. It stops me in my tracks sometimes when I think about him or just stare at him. He's so amazing, so funny, so gorgeous, and knowing how much my mum loved babies and kids, and how she would've had a grandson, I just know she would've gone a bit crazy for him. So, I want Lucky to know that, and I'll make sure he knows it every day.

CHAPTER TEN

The love I've been able to experience for Lucky has been life changing. It's a different kind of love, one I've never felt before, and I know everyone says that, but it's true. It's overwhelming, that's the perfect word for it, because I can't control it, and I find myself living for Lucky now.

I care more for him than I do about my own wellbeing and that kind of love takes over you. It's something I've been shocked by because I never anticipated it. The power of my love for him will often scare me and make me sad. I'll be sitting there getting emotional at the thought of him growing up and leaving home, or going to school, or another child being nasty to him and Lucky being upset.

I've just been flooded with emotions. Sometimes I

think, if anything happens to him, that will be my life as well, and that feeling is daunting and scary, but it's also beautiful because I'm lucky to have someone that I love that much. I can't imagine living my life without my son, and so it haunts me when I think about Nan losing her Jonathan. I don't understand how she's gone on to be the woman she is, so happy and grateful after the loss of two children. It's just so shocking.

From time to time, Nan and I have spoken about Jonathan, especially because his birthday (the 16th August) happens to be the same day as Fizz's, which is so spooky to me, and often on that day Nan will mention how old he would've been. To be honest, it's quite sad because sometimes my grandparents will look at Lucky and say he reminds them of their son, who was also a blonde, beautiful little boy. I've seen my granddad cry looking at Lucky because he's reminded of the little boy he lost.

I know a lot of mothers experience those flashes of fear about something happening to their children, and that we have to work extra hard to rationalise those terrifying thoughts, all while trusting in life. The older Lucky gets, the more used to these feelings I become, but other feelings take their place, like me being critical of myself.

Sometimes when I drop him off at nursery, I feel a bit of relief because I get some time to myself. Then I feel guilty for having those feelings, which I know are quite normal. It's easy to question all these things in my head, and to wonder if I'm doing enough, but I've had to tell myself that I'm everything that Lucky needs, and that's why being a mum is so special.

The best part is that I'm someone's everything. I'm Lucky's safe space and knowing that is really comforting. I also feel like I can appreciate that more after losing Mum. Becoming one myself has replaced something in my heart that I thought was lost when Mum passed away. I know how much Lucky needs me, and I get to be that person for him, and there's something about that bond that steps in for the mother-daughter relationship that I lost.

For me, there's always been a beauty in creating life and bringing children up. I've craved having a big family since the beginning because that's the situation I grew up in, and being one of seven shaped who I am and how my life's unfolded. If I didn't have my siblings around me after all we've been through, I don't know how life would've been manageable.

Reflecting on things now, I want a big family, but if I'm honest, probably not as big as I once thought. I used to want five kids, but my feelings have changed a bit after having just one. Now I struggle with the thought of sharing my love between that many children. Even just having another one makes me nervous because I'm scared of halving my love between Lucky and another child. People say that having another child simply expands your heart, and that a new part of your heart develops for the new one, so perhaps when I'm feeling more confident, I'll be ready to have a second child. But I know I'm still scared by the things I've experienced because there's always another part of me that feels like I don't want to push my luck, that if I do, something bad might happen, so I'm really aware of that. I want to be able to look after and nurture my children, and to be honest, the thought of making sure my kids are all healthy and happy, especially if I have five, just seems daunting. So now, I think that I'd be happy just to have a couple of healthy children that I can look after and give all my love to.

Watching Lucky grow up has already been bittersweet. I'm watching him hit these milestones and flourish but at the same time, I'm losing my baby boy. He's eighteen months old now and walking, pretty much running I'd say. He's literally pulling his arms back and charging forward these days. He's got a lot of energy.

He's babbling a lot now, too, and right from early on, I made sure Lucky's first word was 'Mama'. I was drilling it into him until he started saying, 'Mamamama'. But I got my payback on that one because now all he's saying is, 'Daddy Daddy Daddy'!

As soon as Lucky hit one, time seemed to just fly

by as life picked back up again, after a relatively quiet first six months. It's been so special watching his little personality come out. He's very cheeky and very funny, even at such a young age. He can't really speak yet, but you can just tell he's a little performer. Everyone says it! It's like he just wants to make people laugh, and he thrives on it, so when he's doing something and people are entertained, he'll do it even more.

I just love his confidence. He's not afraid to walk into a room and put on a show for everyone. It's nice for me to see that because I know I was quite introverted as a child. I love how he's blossoming and hope that carries on as he gets older.

*

Since having Lucky, my relationship with Lewis has grown stronger, allowing me to think more long-term. Before Lewis, I never used to be bothered about getting married, and I went through a stage of being quite cynical about being with someone forever. I was scared by everything that I'd been through, and my mentality was that nothing lasts forever, and no one sticks around. Mum had died. Fizz had died. And my parents' marriage hadn't worked out.

I even said these thoughts aloud to Lewis at the start of our relationship, and it used to upset him a bit. But as my relationship deepened, and after Lucky came along,

I thought, *Why can't it be forever? I want it to be, so why not start believing it's possible?* It's not like I didn't have any examples of long-term relationships – after all Nan and Granddad have stayed married for some 50 odd years, and I love when Nan tells the story of how they met. She was 14 years old and working part-time during the summer holidays at a cafe in a motorway service area in Pontefract, north of Doncaster. My grandad, who was 16, was working at the same place but as a wine waiter in the posh restaurant area. He went to the local grammar school for boys, and she went to the local grammar school for girls, and they discovered there was only a week's difference in their October birthdays. Apparently, it was love at first sight and they got married in 1969 when they were in their early 20s. They've been together ever since, so I know true and long love can exist. Lewis has given me faith in that.

When Lewis proposed to me on the 3rd November 2023, it was totally unexpected. Only a few weeks before, we'd spoken about getting engaged the following year with a wedding the year after because of the money we'd spent renovating the house. But Lewis had been planning the occasion all along, and he threw me off guard in the most beautiful of ways.

Lewis is naturally very romantic, and even without trying he does little things that make me feel special, something I'd never experienced before in my past relationships. I know it sounds cringey to say, but everyday he'll tell me that I'm beautiful, and it's just nice especially when you can tell someone means it. Even when we're waking up in the morning, and I don't exactly feel fresh, he'll be like, 'Oh you look beautiful today.'

Our love languages are quite different, so whereas he's someone who always wants me near, and very much loves physical touch, I'm the type of person who enjoys acts of service, little things, but I feel our languages complement each other quite nicely.

On the day of the proposal, Lewis told me to pack a bag for the weekend because we were hopping on the Eurostar. As I said, he's very much like this, very giving and spontaneous, and he also works in travel, so I didn't think too much of it. He didn't tell me where we were going, but I knew it had to be either Paris or Amsterdam, maybe even Belgium. I suspected Paris though because we love it, but I also thought, *We've been a few times already, so maybe it's somewhere else.*

We were taking Lucky with us as usual, so there wasn't really an indication that this needed to be an occasion for Mommy and Daddy. It's hard for Lewis and me to prioritise date nights because we genuinely love having Lucky with us. We enjoy family time so much and don't mind putting all our focus on him when we're out, where he's wanting entertainment and our full attention. But when we do prioritise date nights, we get a lot out of it, and know it's not just important for us, but for Lucky too.

Anyway, the three of us were going away somewhere mysterious, and eventually we arrived in Paris. We took a taxi to this amazing five-star hotel called Le Bristol, and that evening, Lewis told me he had a surprise for me.

'I'll take Lucky and you get ready,' he said.

As I was doing my makeup, I filmed a little content for TikTok, a 'Get ready with me for the first night in Paris' kind of thing, not knowing what was about to happen. Meanwhile, Lewis kept texting, asking me if I was ready so he could come back up and get me.

Nearly there … I texted back, obviously taking forever with my tutorial. *He's acting a bit shady*, I thought, but I didn't think too much of it. When Lewis came back to the room again, Lucky in his arms, he asked again, 'Are you ready yet?'

'Yeah … I just need to pack my handbag.'

'You won't need that.'

'*Well*, I will … I need my makeup bits.'

'No, you won't need that,' he repeated. 'Just come with me.'

I'd noticed a door in our hotel room that was locked when we first checked in, and Lewis had told me quite casually that we could book it as a conjoining room, if we needed to. Now he was taking me to this mysterious room through another door and saying, 'You know how much I love you, don't you?' We walked in and the first thing I saw were rose petals on the floor, and I thought, *What the hell is going on?* Then I saw a staff lady trying to shove back up a balloon that said, 'Marry Me' on it, which had fallen from the ceiling. She was simultaneously trying to film the whole thing because Lewis knew I'd want this filmed. As soon as I read that balloon, I started shouting, 'Oh my God!', just so excited, while Lewis was all nervous and flustered, and Lucky was trying to wriggle out of his hands.

The whole thing was perfectly imperfect and quite funny. Then when Lewis got down on one knee and asked me to marry him, I immediately replied, 'Yes!', and started jumping around. I was so, so happy.

Lucky had no idea what was going on. You can see him in the video picking up rose petals and wondering what they were. Afterwards, we all went down to the bar. Lewis and I had a few glasses of wine, and we were buzzing with excitement before we headed for a nice meal. I'd never heard of the engagement bubble before this, but now I know it's definitely a real thing.

I didn't know how much the engagement would mean to me, but I really felt complete. It became one of those moments I'd relive again and again. Lewis and I have been together now for close to four years, and what we have now is just really special. Everything we've created so far, in such a short span of time, speaks to our amazing connection, our bond, the way we trust and support each other.

We had this undeniable connection from the word go, came up against so many hurdles together and overcame them, and stuck with each other through everything. It's not been easy or straightforward, and in fact, it's something we both had to work hard at. But in the end, I'd say it was all worth it.

CHAPTER ELEVEN

Lewis and I thought we'd be able to have the house completed within nine months and that everything would fall into place with the three of us moving into our amazing space. But we didn't end up moving until Lucky was one year old, with the entire project taking 18 months to complete. I wouldn't have had it any other way though, and I do honestly feel it was all meant to be.

Now that we're all settled in our new home, it was totally worth the wait. I think about how I created our home from scratch, and how I created it for my family, and I'm just so proud. The delay on the house made us appreciate it so much more. Lewis and I could've had our own time in it, but when we found out our little boy was on the way, it made us want to work even harder.

It also made me want to create the perfect house, not just for me and Lewis, but for our new family.

Looking back, it's all worked out how it was meant to be, and everything in my life simply goes back to that one word: lucky. I feel like people think I'm just saying it, but I genuinely mean it. I feel lucky and I know that I am.

When Lucky was born, I worried that I might have to give up parts of my career, something I'd worked hard to build, because I couldn't imagine leaving him for a day of shooting or a meeting or whatnot. I wanted to stay and protect this little bundle of joy that I loved more than anything.

I spent the first few weeks thinking that until I thought, *I love him so much I want to go out and work and do well for him so that I can give him the life he deserves.* I wanted to carry on with work to show him what it looked like to be ambitious and go out and get what you want, a bit like what I did for the big twins, when I decided it was time to leave Doncaster after Mum died.

I went straight back to work when Lucky was about two weeks old but that's just what I'm like. Because I'd done up the house, and it cost me more than I thought it would, I wanted to catch up on time and money lost. After everything I've been through, it's always been my natural impulse to carry on with work. I still had contracts with brands requiring monthly posts, so I still needed to shoot content, which was quite hard after giving birth because I didn't feel myself physically and mentally. Yet I never wanted to miss out on a good job or making money just because I didn't feel that good within myself, so I just got on with it.

I remember working with a brand who had contracted me to post underwear, but because they had pyjamas in their range, I managed to tailor a few of my posts to wear that instead. Like I said before, I knew how to adapt. A couple of months had passed, and they still wanted me to pose in their underwear. So, I let go of my insecurities and posted a video reel. There was no editing, just my real body. There was no posing, just me in a bra and knickers showing my postpartum body to the world. It felt freeing. I had to own the fact that I'd just had a baby and didn't need to have a flat stomach or be toned straight away. No one expected that from me, and I knew this, but I guess I expected that from myself. The post got a lot of engagement, that's for sure, and it helped a lot of women relate to having a postpartum body.

About three weeks or so after giving birth, I turned to Lewis and told him I needed to get back into shape again. I'd struggled to accept my new body throughout and then after the pregnancy, so when I had the energy to, I was determined to get back into shape.

I've always enjoyed fitness, but I couldn't really train

the same while pregnant, so I was excited to get that fitness back and get my body back as well. The feelings I had towards my new body were ruining my experience of motherhood, and I wanted to feel healthy, energised and happy for Lucky so I could be a good mum to him.

I know there's a lot of women who don't want to put that kind of pressure on themselves, accepting their body as it is after such a gruelling experience, and that's fine, but for *me*, I needed and wanted to get back into shape because that's what would ultimately make *me* happy. A lot of people were quick to judge my comments online about wanting to lose weight so quickly, or how I chose to express how I felt within my body, but after nine months of carrying Lucky and going through an enormous transformation, and after nine months of eating foods full of sugar and nothing nutritious, I was ready to make a change and get back to how I used to be.

Lewis knew a good trainer in the area, and he suggested we go and see him together and do a few sessions, and I could see how I felt after that. And that's how our fitness journey started, and how Verdure was eventually born.

I honestly don't know how I had the strength to train straight away, bearing in mind I had a three-week-old new-born. I was able to take up some light exercise after that time as I'd had an uncomplicated and natural birth – if I'd had a C-section or suffered complications, the recovery time would've been much longer, about six weeks.

Of course, though, every woman will have their own individual timeframe for when they're allowed to start working out again and how gentle or strenuous it should be. When my own midwife gave me the okay during my postnatal check-up, I was ready to get going, and once I get something in my head, nothing can stop me. This is probably where the nature of my work actually helped. The reality of my situation is that I'm in the business of trends, of fashion, of makeup and beauty. It's my passion, but it's also part of my brand, so it was important for me to get back to a place where I felt comfortable and good about myself.

A lot of my work would've stopped tomorrow if I hadn't got into shape and looked after myself, but I also wanted to do it for me. My job requires me to be aware of and stick with trends to stay relevant, and it's something I've struggled with because I also like what I like so it often takes me a bit of time to jump into the next trend.

It's the same with the filler. It took me so long to come out of that trend because everyone else was coming off it, but I couldn't because I was stuck in it. Fashion trends are the same way. Overall, I try and have a balance between keeping with the trends and being true to myself because I never want it to seem like I'm trying too hard. It's not authentic that way. But at the end of the day, brands want to work with people who are following the trends, or dressing a certain way, or have a particular look. I could only show off my postpartum body for so long before I'd need to work hard to return to my usual weight.

Because I started training and eating well, I thought I could turn my weight loss around in three months, but it ended up taking a full year. Lewis and I saw the trainer three times a week, and because the trainer was also a nutritionist, he put us on a meal plan. He initially told us we couldn't eat any carbs, and at first I thought, *Nope, can't do this ... no carbs? Absolutely not.* But I changed my mind after I started seeing the effects.

The entire journey was an up and down one emotionally. I'd lose the weight and think my body was back, and then another month would go by only to realise I still had a lot of work to do. The weight kept falling off, but the journey would take time and I needed to be patient with myself, learning to accept the highs and lows. I lost the weight after six or seven months, but I needed to tone up for another three to four, and throughout the whole process I learned that my body is a lot stronger than I thought it was, and that I'd managed to build strength that I didn't know I had.

I also realised that there are so many different diets out there, but for me, limiting carbs and processed foods, and prioritising natural foods works well. Lewis and I don't see ourselves as being on a diet. It's more that we've made a lifestyle choice. We enjoy the types of food we eat now because they make us feel energised instead of sluggish. It's also nice not to fall into the trap of binge eating anymore or seeking diets that ultimately cause you to backtrack and eat poorly.

If we fancy it, we'll enjoy the odd treat, and won't beat ourselves up about it, and we're much more aware now of the types of ingredients that are in certain foods. That also comes with being a mum and realising the importance of foods that are nutritious for the body. The way we look after our health is very important for me now, and amidst it all, we just want to be as mentally and physically fit as we can for Lucky.

There wasn't much focus put on health when I was growing up, not in a bad way, we just ate quite normally because that's all my mum knew. Once I started travelling, I also realised how we were never exposed to certain foods up north. It might sound odd, but I never used to eat fish and certainly not food like sushi, which I didn't even know was a thing. Being from a small town, we didn't have access to a lot of different kinds of foods, especially as a working-class family. I used to be quite fussy growing up, so these days my family can't believe how I eat. Even Nan – there's no way you'd catch her eating raw fish. She won't eat any of it.

If someone had said to me before my fitness journey that it would take a year to get my body back, I would've grown quite upset, but looking back I'm proud of what I've accomplished. I feel better in my body and my mind, but I've also set up a new habit and routine for life, managing to hit the gym at least five days a week.

I learned more than what I knew before, not just about fitness but nutrition too, and I just got obsessed with it. Lewis and I ended up learning so much that we decided to partner up with our trainer and launch an app. It's always been important for me to move with the times and study the trends, so building upon something new that I was passionate about seemed like the right thing to do.

These days I feel so much healthier, and it's been nice to channel my passion for what I've learned into a new project. I launched the fitness and wellness app at the start of 2024, so the business had been a couple of years in the making and stemmed from my followers wanting to know how I managed to lose the almost four stone I'd gained during my pregnancy. Once I felt ready, I remember posting a before and after picture of myself online a year after the transformation, and the reactions I received were crazy.

It seemed some of my followers were in the same position where maybe they'd had a baby and wanted to lose those extra pounds, or more generally wanted to make a change in their lifestyle. The demand seemed to be there to show how I transformed my body, so the businesswoman in me thought, *Right, why not make an app where I can offer what I've learned and give people a way to join me on the journey?*

The idea came at the perfect time, and I guess the physical journey of pregnancy offered me that new inspiration. And these days, I'm not as heavily involved in Tanologist, so I made Verdure into a new venture I could really throw myself into.

My role in Tanologist centred around being the face of a product, marketing the product, and testing the product while everything else had been set up already. I knew that once it was time to start a new business, I'd want to start from scratch and build something I had more control over, allowing me to make the big decisions and be more involved in the backend stuff.

Since I started Verdure (which is another word for health and a feeling of strength), my knowledge around business has expanded, which has been quite useful. The app will continue to develop and grow, but at the minute I've introduced the 'Lottie Programme' that includes a three-month fitness programme. I filmed all the workouts myself, so my subscribers can train with me as they're working out to get in shape. There's also a nutrition section which includes loads of healthy recipes, and most importantly there's a community section where everyone can chat and post in the feed and spur each other on.

On my own journey, it was so important having Lewis there to train with me for that additional support, and it was quite helpful having a personal trainer to push me to do things I might not have wanted to do. We're already thinking about new programmes to introduce and events we can have in the future to bring people together. It's all very exciting and creative.

It's been a privilege having Lewis as a business partner because we have that built-in trust between us. It's quite a dangerous game sometimes joining forces with some-one you don't know, so being able to work with someone I'm close to eliminates a lot of risk. I'm also just familiar and comfortable working with people that I'm close to, and with Lou, for example, even though we had a working relationship first, we very quickly became amazing friends.

I'm not saying it's all roses working with people you're close to, sometimes it can be quite intense. Sometimes you'll be dealing with differences in opinion and that can be harder to navigate with someone you know well, so it's a privilege but also comes with its own challenges. I think you've got to make sure that if you do go into business with someone that you're close to, that you go into it with a similar goal in mind otherwise there could be friction.

Lewis and I are very open with each other, and if our working relationship ever got to a point where it was causing any issues between us, we wouldn't do it. Our priority is always our relationship, so as long as we're enjoying our working relationship then we'll carry on.

One of many things I appreciate though when it comes to working with him is how he drives me to do stuff that I'm more apprehensive or nervous about. I wanted to start Verdure, but I was also naturally doubtful, wondering whether I'd get the subscribers and all that stuff, but Lewis was always right behind me, encouraging me to just do it and giving me the confidence to do so.

*

When I spoke about happiness at the beginning of the book, and what it all means to me, it centred on what I've created in my life since all the loss – my relationship with Lewis, focusing on Lucky, working hard on projects and new ventures, and the quality time I spend with family. Travelling and exploring new places (now with Lewis and Lucky) has continued to be a passion, and Lewis and I work hard to prioritise our next destination. So far as a family we've been to Paris, Marrakech, Dubai and the Maldives.

For me, I love the *ritual* around travelling – packing my bags, going to the airport, boarding and flying –

it gives me more satisfaction sometimes than the actual trip. Despite all the places we've been so far, Lewis and I always say our special place is Ibiza. We go every summer, and we just love the vibe. I don't know what it is, but as soon as I step out of the airport and onto the island, I feel this electric energy. I can't compare Ibiza to any other place. Even before Lewis and I got together, I'd go to Ibiza every summer from when I was 18 years old. That was the start of my rave stage, which probably lasted until just before my 21st birthday.

Sounds funny to say it now, but I got into all the techno rave music back then with Brits. We used to book a hotel, get the train up to Manchester, and go out to places like the Warehouse Project. We went to raves in Ibiza too. When I teamed up with the fashion brand In The Style in 2019, and released my own collection, it was inspired by the rave scene on the island. I'd probably die now looking back on the clothing I created because it's so not me now, but at the time, I thought the collection was sick, what with all the rainbow print and bright Lycra, stuff I absolutely loved back then.

The gig was a lot of fun, and we ended up doing a trip to Ibiza to launch the collection with a group of influencers. At the time I couldn't believe I'd get to go to Ibiza and rave as part of my job. I was buzzing and thinking the whole time, *How is this work?*

Since my pregnancy with Lucky, I've realised it's not

just the partying that drew me to the place, even though I loved going and experiencing the nightlight there. When I was pregnant, I remember asking Lewis if it was still possible to go for the summer, and we just thought, *Why not? Let's just try it.*

We had an amazing experience and saw a completely different side of the island. We could truly see how naturally beautiful it was. And then, the first time we took Lucky, we had a wonderful trip, and did loads of kid friendly stuff. I never would've thought to go to Ibiza with a baby when I was younger, but we discovered it was possible. We've even taken our families, including my Nan and Granddad, which was so special because flying and going abroad fills Nan with absolute horror.

My grandparents have always been quite content with just having a lovely home and being there for us grandchildren, and because my granddad has mobility issues, travelling and going on holiday comes with a lot of fuss, as Nan puts it. She finds travelling difficult even with a wheelchair for Granddad and the mobility help at the airport, but I was able to convince Nan to come out with us and told her not to worry about it. I loved being able to take them away and have a big family holiday together, and I know Nan appreciates it and it feels like we're giving her what she gave to us. It was nice having them around, and when the rest of us wanted to go and have a little night out to relive our party days, they stayed in and looked after Lucky. I've come to see the island now as a more versatile place full of special memories. And hopefully we'll be able to have our dream wedding there, too, where we can celebrate with all our family and friends.

Phoebe's a mum now, which is so nice to see as I know it's something she's always wanted from the age of about 15. Because I'd already had Lucky, I was able to answer the questions she had during pregnancy and after giving birth, and I was happy to be able to give that to her and make life a bit easier for her.

Those first few days after giving birth to Olive, I was able to help her with the baby blues, something she also didn't realise could happen. These days, Phoebe and Olive sometimes come down to stay with me, which means we get to do cute things like bathe the little ones together. I took a picture of that moment once and put it up on Instagram with the caption, 'Our mum would be smiling,' and I just knew how happy Mum would be to see us both in that moment with our kids. It's how we were brought up, so family-orientated, so nurturing and maternal, just wanting to take care of something precious. It's nice to have my sister experiencing motherhood alongside me.

As much as Daisy loves new babies, and gets tempted when she sees Lucky and Olive, she's not ready to have one yet and wants to work a lot first. And then, of course, Brits has a baby now, too, so she's been coming to me for advice, admitting she didn't know how to do a nappy before I showed her. It's nice when friends can grow alongside each other, and now that we're raising children together, our relationship has deepened even more. Now we can do little trips with our babies, but still have a girls' night out. We can't wait for our babies to grow up and be good friends themselves. We can see it all so clearly when Lucky does cute things like push Nola around in his pram.

My dream of wanting (at least one of) my sisters to move down to London has happened, which is so good. As far as Daisy's concerned, we get to see a lot of each other as she has her own flat just five minutes away from me. The two of us love it in London and sometimes enjoy the nightlife together especially for work events. Phoebe still lives up north – she's more of a homebird and always has been. Daisy and I are always asking her to come down for a few days to stay, but she doesn't like the city life too much.

The big twins are establishing their own identities now and have moved away from doing work together as twins to making it on their own. While Phoebe likes the social media side of things, Daisy enjoys modelling more, although she's always loved learning too. Her favourite subject at school was sociology, and her GCSE results were really good, so if the influencing stuff fizzles out for her, she's thinking of going back to study sociology or law.

Louis' still focusing on his music and spends a lot of time in Los Angeles as he has a little boy there. But we make sure to spend the big holiday's together like Christmas (Louis' birthday is the 24th December, so that ties in nicely) and birthdays, where we all meet back home at Nan's. Doris and Ernie I tend to see once a month now. It's been harder to see them since having Lucky, but we're always FaceTiming and texting, which I adore!

As a family, we all have an awareness of how short life can be, which makes us love so much harder. That's the positive that comes out of all this heartbreak. We were always close, but it's made us more protective of each other and so loving.

The way we've come together and maintained our closeness was the most natural way for it all to have moved forward since losing Mum and Fizz, Nan says. From her perspective, it's like we knew, instinctively, that we needed to keep our bond and our family unit tight and impenetrable. We're all very affectionate now, and so touchy-feely, and it's nice because we know that when someone's been taken from you too soon, it's easier to think, *I just want to give them one more hug, I just want to show them I love them one more time*.

Having said that, the funniest thing is that the big

twins don't hug each other at all. They mean the world to each other and tell each other everything, but as Daisy explains, there's something about hugging each other that feels too strange because they're identical twins. She came across something on the internet about it all and felt relieved to see that she and Phoebe weren't the only ones to feel that way. Louis even made a comment about them not hugging once, after Fizz died. He asked if they were going to give each other a hug at any point, but they weren't feeling it. They'll hug all the rest of us, but they won't hug each other, and I guess it's just a twin thing. So that's what my family do now with each other since the losses, and even in my own relationship with Lewis and Lucky, I can never cuddle them too much or kiss them too much because I know that things can change quickly, and I don't want to have any regrets.

For those wondering about our wedding plans, Lewis and I haven't put any in place because we're wondering whether we should have another baby first. The idea of turning around a wedding for next summer would be too soon and it'd be nice to enjoy our engagement a bit more. We also thought that if we left having a second child until after next summer, the age gap between Lucky and the new-born would be too much.

It's hard to plan these things, and I just know that if we put a date in for next summer, I'd fall pregnant straight away. I know I would – stuff like that always happens to me, and I don't want to be pregnant on my wedding day or only have a few months to get myself back in shape. So, I'm leaning towards biting the bullet and having another baby first. I love the thought of doing it all over again – of finding out the baby's sex, carrying my child, feeling him or her move around inside me, and then giving birth – it's truly the most amazing experience.

Of course, there's nerves after my first experience because I know what it takes now, and I know how hard it is mentally and physically. I know I've got to be prepared for all the work I've put into my body to be reversed. But I also know I can do it all again, and the way I see it, having a second child, and giving Lucky a sibling, will be quite a nice break for me. Since having Lucky, I went straight back to work, trained hard and changed how I ate, so I know that once I'm pregnant again, I'll have the tools to make better choices with my food – that's not to say I won't treat myself (I obviously will) but I want to be more conscious about my decisions so it's not as mentally and physically taxing the second time around.

EPILOGUE

When I said at the beginning that it's the simple things that make me happy, like being with my partner, Lewis, and my little boy, Lucky, I meant it. I cherish our family holidays so much, being able to escape for a bit of rest and relaxation. The white sandy beaches, palm trees and blue skies are lovely, but nothing beats spending quality time with my boys. Lewis and I having that chance to love Lucky, and seeing Lucky laugh and smile, melts my heart.

That trip especially, taken just after Phoebe gave birth to Olive, was the first holiday where Lucky was really playing and understanding it and getting so much pleasure from it. But the first time we ever went to the island was when Lucky was born. We had wanted to go away for ages and were trying to figure out a trip while doing up the house. Our priority was to try and save money, but we craved taking him away, and on occasion, I'm offered trips for free, so we were kind of waiting for something like that to come up. When an amazing offer for the Maldives came up for ten nights, we thought, *Oh my god, this is perfect.* Lucky was about seven months at this point, so his first ever holiday was on a lush island in the Indian Ocean, which is pretty good going for a baby.

The first night we arrived, the three of us went for dinner on the beach. It was a starry night and there was a singer playing emotional music, and I broke down crying at the table. It could've been the combination of the long flight, my hormones and the music (which really evoke those emotions in me), but the only thing I could think about during that dream holiday was, *I wish my mum could see this.*

I don't know if that thought will ever go away for the rest of my life. We had amazing times growing up, but we never thought we'd experience places like this, and she knew how much I wanted to be a mum. Even when my surroundings were so beautiful, even surreal, and I was surrounded by the people I love, there would always be that pang of sadness. But with each trip I take with my family, new memories are created, and photos taken, ones I can put in my special box for safe-keeping.

I can remind myself of all the love I have, and all the love that I'm lucky to feel and experience in this life.

It's been quite freeing and emotional writing this book because it's helped me go places that I probably haven't gone to before.

In therapy, I was asked about my feelings and emotions around the deaths of Mum and Fizz, but in writing this book, I've had to relive and remember those painful moments again, which only goes to show the grief journey doesn't necessarily end, it just gets more manageable as time goes on. Processing grief can't be rushed. It has its own timeframe, and it looks different for everyone. You could be dealing with grief for a year, or you could be dealing with grief for ten years. Unfortunately, there's no limit. When going through such tragedy, you bury it quite deep to cope, so each time I read and reread my words, it hit home more than ever before just how much I've experienced in my life, all by the age of 25.

This entire book has hit me with deep emotion and has shown me quite clearly the reality of my life so far. I never thought growing up that I'd suffer through losing my mum and my baby sister, Fizz, so early in life, or that I'd be writing a book about it and still feeling such intense emotions. Naturally, there's been deep sadness in my life, but there's also been true happiness, and all of it has taken me by surprise.

Throughout it all, I'm proud of where I've got to, not just in my life, but also *here*, with this book, as it's not been easy having to go into every detail of the worst moments I've ever faced. From day one, my goal has always been to help people experiencing grief, to be a voice, to be a small support – it's what inspired me to work with Sue Ryder, and it's what encouraged me to write this book, so hopefully being able to do that makes it all worthwhile. Anyone who decided to pick up this book, thank you. I really hope you were able to take something away from it, no matter how big or small.

I wanted this book to be positive and uplifting. But I also needed to be honest about the journey I've been through. We all have to deal with sad and difficult moments in life – they're inescapable, a part of what it means to be truly alive. I wanted to be transparent and open, to show that without darkness, you can't have the light.

Like I said before, I consider myself lucky (*again, that word lucky*) that I have such a brilliant family to lean on when times are tough. I consider myself lucky to have the most amazing partner and best friend in Lewis, and that I have my son, Lucky, who I love more than anything. I consider myself lucky that I have a career and a passion that's given me something to put my focus on. These things have given me a reason to keep going, to see the good in life.

It's been amazing reflecting on my achievements and giving thanks to those who helped me along the way. Many of us don't do that enough – we don't look back at our accomplishments and actually appreciate how far we've come, so it's lovely to acknowledge that.

In many ways, losing Mum and Fizz has allowed me to know what true gratitude means. When I was younger, I never used to think about gratitude, and I took everything for granted, something that's easy for us to do. But I've learned that if you're not grateful for what you already have, no new blessings can come into your life. I make it a practice now to be grateful for what I've got. I think when you lose people it becomes even more important.

Looking back, I never realised how truly special Mum was – like I knew it and I felt it, but I couldn't see how fortunate I was to have her be so present, and loving, and caring. When I lost her, it became impossible not to be struck with that feeling of gratitude for everything she brought into my life, and everything else I have, including Lucky and my family. I always say to Lewis, *No matter what we do, as long as we've got each other, as long as we've got our house and a roof over our heads, everything else is a bonus.* It might sound a bit cringey, I know, but before I go to sleep, I thank the Universe for my son and for Lewis. The last thing I think at night is just *Please keep them safe, and if nothing else, I just want Lucky to live a long and healthy life.* That's what I think every night before I fall asleep, that's all I ever want, nothing else. In many ways, it's like I'm praying to my mum, believing she's watching over us, protecting us. These are the things I hold onto, otherwise it's too easy to live in fear, and that's not a way to live. I'm hopeful that after everything I've been through that's my tragedy out the way. I'm really excited for what's next... and feeling so lucky.

ACKNOWLEDGEMENTS

Of course, my best friend & fiancé Lewis, I would not have been able to do this without you. Thank you. My beautiful baby boy Lucky for making me who I am today. I adore you both forever.

To my whole family for being the most important people in my life and the most amazing support. Nan, Grandad, Dad & Sallie, Phoebe & Daisy, Louis and Doris and Ernie. I love you all so much!

To my amazing ghost writer, Jennifer Obidike, for making the experience so nice and for being so gentle.

To Kate Evans for believing in this since day one and helping me get things off the ground! You've been amazing.

To my amazing agent Kirsty for making this happen and being so supportive along the way.

To the whole lovely team at Bonnier! Susannah Otter, Ciara Lloyd, Natalia Cacciatore, Clare Kelly and Charlotte Brown.

To the lovely Karis Kennedy for shooting my cover.